Our Special
Child

Thank you!

Judy Quate

Our Special Child

Jason's Story

Judith Iris Quate

TATE PUBLISHING
AND ENTERPRISES, LLC

Published by Tate Publishing & Enterprises, LLC
127 E. Trade Center Terrace | Mustang, Oklahoma 73064 USA
1.888.361.9473 | www.tatepublishing.com

Tate Publishing is committed to excellence in the publishing industry. The company reflects the philosophy established by the founders, based on Psalm 68:11,
"The Lord gave the word and great was the company of those who published it."

Book design copyright © 2015 by Tate Publishing, LLC. All rights reserved.
Cover design by Junriel Boquecosa
Interior design by Jomel Pepito

Published in the United States of America

ISBN: 978-1-63418-036-8
1. Family & Relationships / Children With Special Needs
2. Self-Help / General
14.12.20

There are two groups on Facebook I follow dedicated to the needs of cerebral palsy parents. It is my extreme pleasure to dedicate this book to the Cerebral Palsy Parents Information and Cerebral Palsy Support Group Our Hidden Treasures.

To all parents of special needs children, I dedicate this book to you as well. My heart and soul go out to you all.

Acknowledgments

Before Jason was born, I would have described myself as an introverted, shy young woman. I had difficulty making friends and keeping them. Apparently, God saw a potential in me I didn't know I possessed. He gave me Jason and Michael. They both gave me a reason and a purpose to become an extrovert and with this new personality, how to advocate for their needs. I did it well. I worked hard to get the best education, help find the best medical care available, and become a good mom for which I am most proud of.

Because of God's gift to me, I became an outgoing, determined woman/mother/wife who understood how to advocate for my children. Having Michael in my life made me whole. Having Jason in my life made me understand the gift I was given.

There were so many people who were part of Jason's life in some way, either brief or long term. They deserve my esteem appreciation for their contributions in being part of Jason's community and helping him grow. Please know I appreciate the connection you had with Jason and I thank you from the bottom of my heart.

My dear husband and father of our children, Allen, held our family together during the hard times and always worked very hard keeping food on our table while I stayed home to care for the boys. He is and was a great dad to Michael and Jason. He played with both boys equally without treating Jason as a "fragile" child. So many times through the years, I was told it was very apparent Jason came from a happy and loving family who taught him how to love. This is why he had his "signature" smile. I know his dad had a lot to do with this. To my dear husband, always know you are a wonderful dad to Michael and you were a special dad to Jason. For this, I am eternally blessed and full of love for the special man you are.

Michael, you were a great brother to Jason. I know Jason loved you with all his heart. There were many times when you were playing on your own and I placed Jason down on the floor with you. He would lay there watching you and attempt to reach out to touch you. It was his way of showing his love for you. Through the years, you never hesitated to join us when we visited him monthly. You never hesitated to stop whatever you were doing when Jason was rushed to a hospital. You were right by his side at the hospital to support him. Most importantly, I see compassion and sensitivity within your soul because of having a brother with special needs. You now have a family of your own with two beautiful children. You were blessed to have Jason as a brother.

To my dear sister Arlene, there are no words to express how much I love you and how proud I am to have you as my sister. You were there for me from the day the boys were born until Jason's death and beyond. You also experienced difficulty in your life. However, when I called you to vent my feelings, you were always there for me. Who could have guessed as young children with normal sibling rivalries, we end up being best friends and loving sisters.

I am so blessed to have had a great extended family who accepted Jason as "normal" that includes Frank and Jean Quate (Allen's parents), Milton and Sarah Lax (my parents), and my brother-in-law, Paul Wattman. They all passed away, and I miss them so very much. I don't know how I survived without their support. My brother-in-law was our family poet. He would write a poem in fifteen minutes, if needed, for a last-minute occasion. He wrote the following poem in memory of Jason and read it at his funeral. I am honored to share it with you here.

My nephew Jason has been taken away
And now he's up in heaven and there he will stay.
He's had a hard life ever since he was born
And I feel my heart has been broken since he has gone.
You see even though he couldn't walk or speak
He was much stronger than he was weak.
We used to go see him at the home every once in a while
And he would light up a room with his great smile.
He made it to Bubby's 80s birthday part in May
And he really made her day.
We'll miss you and love you and that's all I have to say
And now it's time for God to take you away.

To my dear nephew and niece, Barry and Rena, who were more than cousins, they were brother and sister to my boys. Rena, I don't know what I would have done without your help. You provided me a sense of security walking Michael home from school every day while I was working. Thank you, guys, with all my heart! You both loved Jason unconditionally.

Nancy, fate brought us together and love will keep us as friends for eternity. We have and had a special bond that will never be broken. Jason and Abby are now in heaven together and reunited their special friendship.

To all the doctors, therapists, caregivers, and the staff at Skills of Central PA, what would I have done without you? I needed your support and help, and I am forever in your debt. Jason was especially lucky to have two families who loved and cared for him. What more can I ask for?

There were two doctors in Jason's life who were so special to Jason and me. They certainly deserve recognition, Lawrence

Brown, MD and Lee Segal, MD. You both treated Jason and I with dignity and respect, and I will forever be grateful.

To all our friends and neighbors, thank you with all my heart for your support, love, and for loving Jason unconditionally. This especially includes the Wendeler family—Jaqueline, Karl, Paula, and Michael and their friends who were special in so many ways, Maureen and Lisa. I would be remiss if I didn't mention Lisa's devotion to Jason that guided her future to teaching special education at the early intervention level. This is an example how Jason changed people's lives by just knowing him.

Meladye, when I met you that first day, I had no clue as to your dedication and involvement in Jason's life. Jason fell "in love" for the first time when he met you. I saw it in his eyes. He flirted with you every time I saw you two together. You two had a special bond. I realized it recently, when you cried after hearing Jason had passed away. After all the years past, he still affected you. Always know you are a great teacher and please continue to give that special love you have to each of your students the only way you know how.

George, I am so grateful for your friendships through the years. When I needed your support and comfort during the difficult years trying to balance work and caring for Jason, you were there for me, and I will always be grateful.

To Pamela, you are my rock. Many days when I needed a shoulder to cry on, you were there to hold me up and keep my spirits high. You never hesitated to help and guide me through the hard times. I love you for that. Thank you from the bottom of my heart for your commitment to read my manuscript, edit, and make suggestions for changes. You gave me the confidence to keep on with this project when at times I thought it was overwhelming.

To my editor, I thank you from the bottom of my heart for the tedious job you undertook in reading my entire book and your bravery for putting up with my errors and correcting them. Never in my life did I ever believe I would write a book. However, when

Jason was born, my life changed dramatically, so writing a book was a perfect conclusion to a lifelong experience caring for Jason. I did not have experience writing, and I needed a good editor who had the patience to help me. For this, I am forever grateful.

Most importantly, I am so grateful for Tate Publishers for their willingness to take on a new author. Thank you for seeing and understanding why I needed to write Jason's story. I appreciate your support in helping me to achieve my goal to write *Our Special Child: Jason's Story.*

Contents

Introduction

My son Jason lived twenty-eight years in a wheelchair because he was trapped inside a body inflicted with spastic quadriplegic cerebral palsy.

This was Jason's life; we accepted it, and I did everything I could to help him live a life of dignity, comfort, and love.

While reading this book you will learn how special he was and why I felt the strong need to tell his story. There were so many hurdles I had to overcome to get him the support he needed and to provide a comfortable life. He was not mentally retarded. He was considered physically challenged to a degree where he was labeled "retarded." This word is not part of my vocabulary since I consider it to be a vulgar description of a person who is both mentally and physically challenged. I would prefer to use mentally and physically challenged. However, in 1979, when Jason was born, this was the predominant characterization of someone with special challenges. Through the years, many labels used to describe individuals with severe physical and mental challenges were changed to make it more "politically correct."

Mourning my dear son and thinking back at all the problems we overcame as a family, I soon realized how special his life was. I deeply felt the need to share his story to the world. I know Jason would want me to. He is always in my thoughts, and I feel his presence every day.

Prologue

I awoke from my sleep with the need to use the bathroom. It was 1:00 a.m. I suddenly feel a gush of water flowing down my legs. Allen was still sleeping. I quietly approached and whispered, "I think my water bag broke, dear."

Startled from my innocent comment, Allen quickly jumped out of bed and quite abruptly squealed, "Oh no! Not now after everything we went through." He ran downstairs, found the emergency phone number, and dialed. The woman from the answering service reassured Allen she will contact the doctor on call immediately. After five minutes, the phone rang and our doctor calmly told Allen to take me to the Emergency Ward at Albert Einstein Medical Center.

This was the largest hospital located close to our home in Philadelphia. My obstetrician advised me to choose this hospital because the risk involved in delivering twins.

As I was packing my suitcase and preparing to leave for the hospital I was evaluating my calm, passive attitude. "Why am I so calm? I should be in a state of panic, but I am not. I am thinking about all the treatments I endured with Dr. Groll and how I became pregnant three times, two ending in miscarriages. This is our first viable pregnancy. It occurs to me I am not being honest with my feelings. I am pretending to be pregnant as a defense mechanism so if anything should go wrong, I am protecting myself from further anguish. My due date is November 11; today is September 8. The anguish of my life continues, and I refuse to face the consequences."

The Beginning

Allen and I were married in 1971. In 1974, after three blissful years of marriage, we decided to expand our family. I am working as a medical secretary at Albert Einstein Medical Center in Philadelphia, Pennsylvania. This job was offered to me after working three years in the Medical Records Department as a medical transcriptionist. I love my job and love the three doctors I work for.

We tried to get pregnant for a few years. During a routine appointment with my gynecologist, I asked, "Do I need to be concerned? Is it normal to wait this long?"

"You have an unusual history of irregular menstrual cycles and this is the cause of your infertility," he said. "You are not ovulating on a regular basis. You need to ovulate regularly in order for your husband's sperm to reach your egg during ovulation, to form a fetus. Because your ovulation is irregular, your chances of becoming pregnant are almost impossible without treatment. I would like to recommend a specialist. Will you allow me to arrange an appointment for you?"

He made an appointment for me to see Michael Groll, MD. Allen and I entered his office reluctantly, not knowing what to expect.

Dr. Groll listened as I gave him the details of my problem and what my gynecologist explained to me. He listened carefully and took vigorous notes.

He put down his pen and looked up. "I believe I can help you achieve your goal of getting pregnant. I will like to help you if you want me to." He continued, "I treat many women with irregular ovulation problems similar to yours with a very high success rate."

We both looked at each other, and I turned back to Dr. Groll with a feeling of great relief, and said, "Please help us!" Allen agreed by nodding his head.

Dr. Groll picked up the phone and asked his assistant to schedule a few tests for both of us to have. He told us it is important these tests be done to rule out other possible reasons why we are unable to get pregnant.

Allen's tests results were negative. My tests results returned to reveal an irregular hormone blood count that accounts for my irregular menstrual cycles and ovulation.

I returned to Dr. Groll's office alone after receiving the test results. As I was sitting in his office, he told me, "I would like to place you on a regimen of Clomid taken orally and Pergonal, which is dispensed through injection. This combined medication needs to start immediately after your menstruation cycle to build your hormone level to create ovulation. I would like you to take your temperature daily before getting out of bed in the morning and keep a chart to so I can detect the range of your temperature." He continued, "Two weeks after your menstruation and when your temperature chart indicates you are ovulating, this would be the best time to begin trying in order to achieve the best results."

I left his office. I am in the car on my way home thinking, *How technical he sounded. I wondered if it ever occurred to him you cannot turn on emotional passion. The idea of giving us a time slot to have sex takes away everything beautiful about the act of love. It takes away the spontaneity and the romanticism of the act. How can one react positively to a planned activity?* The more my mind was going through all of this, the more I became frustrated and distraught with my thoughts going in so many directions.

Apparently, I underestimated him. I created unnecessary emotional distress. During my next appointment with Dr. Groll, he handed me a wrapped sterilized jar and said, "I would like Allen to provide a sperm sample. When your temperature chart shows you are ovulating, you will come to my office with this sample. I will inseminate his sperm in your cervix, which should travel through to your uterus with the hope it fertilizes your egg. Look at it as a 'backup' plan to give both of you a better chance of achieving positive results."

Okay, now I get it. He does have some compassion! After arriving home that evening, we both discussed the details of the visit. My dear husband is such a trooper. He is more than willing to provide a sample, feeling somewhat humiliated, I am sure.

The day arrived when my temperature chart indicated I was beginning ovulation. Allen gave me a sample of his sperm and I took it with me to work until the time arrived when I needed to leave for Dr. Groll's office. He inseminated Allen's sperm through a tube as he previously described to me in detail.

Two weeks later, we are pregnant after the first session. Unfortunately, our celebration is shortened when I started bleeding. I immediately went down to the hematology department where they took blood from me. Dr. Groll called me later that day and told me I have an unviable pregnancy, and he will schedule me for a Dilatation and Evacuation (D&E).

Two months after our miscarriage, we tried the procedure for the second time. Again, we became pregnant, and again, two days later, I aborted the fetus resulting in another miscarriage.

This is when we decided to give up. We began talking about adoption procedures.

"Because of the extraordinary expense of the drug treatments we already went through, we do not see how we can continue with another treatment." I told Dr. Groll at our next appointment after having another D&E procedure.

"I so strongly believe in the success rate. Please reconsider your decision," he said. "I understand how difficult this is for the two of you and how hard it is financially, but I ask you to please give it one more chance before giving up." Dr. Groll appeared to beg for just one more time.

Again, Allen and I looked at each other, and this time Allen responded, "Okay, one more time."

We continued with the procedure the following month, following the same routine as the last two times. Surprise, we are pregnant again. Unfortunately as with the two previous times, I began to bleed again two days later.

I was upset as I was sitting at my desk trying not to show emotion since there were patients in the office waiting to see the doctor.

As soon as I was able to leave my office, I reluctantly headed to the lab for another blood test. *What is the point having another blood test just to add to my frustrations and emotional stress and anxiety? Isn't it obvious I am having another miscarriage? I am unable to become pregnant, and I need to accept it,* I thought.

Later on in the day trying to concentrate on my work in front of me, the phone rang. Reluctantly, I picked up the receiver and as I predicted, it was Dr. Groll. His vibrant manner on the phone somewhat surprised me when he told me, "Judy, your blood test showed a viable pregnancy. You are not having another miscarriage."

I am attempting to absorb his words to make sense of them since I am so sure he is going to give me bad news again.

"I called the radiology department and requested an emergency ultrasound. Are you able to leave work?" he asked.

"Of course, I will," I answered as I straightened my desk and walked into my boss's office to tell him where I was going. He is so supportive through everything, and he told me to leave and don't worry about anything.

After I arrived home from the hospital after the ultrasound, I was busying myself to keep my mind off of all negative thoughts trying to keep calm. Allen arrived home and grabbed me and exuberantly said, "Honey, we are pregnant! The blood test proves it. Just hang in there. You will see Dr. Groll tomorrow and everything is good."

My mom offered to go with me since Allen is unable to due to a commitment at work. I drove to Dr. Groll's office, and Mom and I were very quiet during the trip. I know she is as nervous as I am. I am so nervous I am running to the bathroom a few times waiting for Dr. Groll to enter his office.

He walked through the door with a smile on his face. *Okay, this is a good sign,* I thought. *Here I am physically sick with my nerves turning my stomach upside down, and he walks into the office smiling.* Did I tell you he can be dramatic at times?

He sat down beside me and said, "Congratulations, Mom, you are going to have twins."

I must have had a look of shock because he took my hand and said, "Don't worry; everything will be just fine."

We both walked out of his office and together found my mom talking to his secretary. "Mom, you may want to sit down while you hear my news." She stares at me looking like she is about to cry when I quickly told her, "I am going to have twins!" I immediately held onto her arm so she would not lose her balance from the look of shock she presented. Mom regained her composure after registering the news she just heard, and immediately grabbed me to express her joy and happiness for me and for our family.

We are on our way home in the car laughing. We are both imagining the look on Allen's face when he hears the news. We were so giddy thinking what his reaction will be.

Immediately, after Allen walks through the door, he anxiously looks at me with fright and terror in his eyes. He saw the smile

on my face and just stared at me in a perplexing way. I decided
to relieve him of his anxiety and simply said, "Hi, Dad of twins!"
I didn't give much thought into my dramatics. I decided to be
straightforward and just spill the beans. I never saw such a shocked
look on his face. After gaining his control, we both laughed with
joy, hugging each other and laughing at the same time.

We still had the issue of bleeding, and Allen asked, "What did
Dr. Groll say about your bleeding?"

"I forgot to ask," I said surprisingly.

However, the next day the bleeding stopped and all is well.

Sadly on January 1, 1986, Dr. Michael Groll was murdered by
a burglar who entered his home, into his bedroom, and murdered
him as he attempted to protect his wife. A very prominent, young
doctor who had a full career ahead of him was gunned down for
no reason at all.

Allen and I were on our way to Albert Einstein Medical
Center. It's two the morning of September 8, 1979. *The streets
are really deserted*, I thought as I sat quietly by Allen side driving
to the hospital. This neighborhood is very familiar to me since I
worked for ten years at Albert Einstein Medical Center before I
was forced to quit when I became pregnant.

We pull up to the emergency ward, parked the car in the
available spot provided for patients, and we both walk through
the doors. An orderly approached with a wheelchair. This was
probably standard procedure when a couple walks in at this time
of the night obviously very pregnant. I was wheeled to a curtained
cubicle where a nurse helped me out of my clothes and into the
standard hospital gown. Our doctor called earlier to inform the
emergency staff I was on my way. She placed an IV in my arm and
sensors on my stomach to monitor the heart rate of my babies.

Dr. Paul arrived. I smiled and thought, *How wonderful; he is my
favorite doctor from the group. Today is my lucky day.* My thought
process during a time of crisis is definitely weird since I was at the
hospital in the seventh month of pregnancy.

He observed the monitor and then listened for their heart beats with his stethoscope. He turned to the nurse and told her somewhat abruptly, "I need Mrs. Quate to have an ultrasound immediately!"

I was returned to my room from having the ultrasound. It appeared the atmosphere of my room changed. Hospital personnel were rushing in and out. Dr. Paul was on the phone speaking quite abruptly to someone, and I was laying there watching everything appear to be falling apart. Dr. Paul returned to me and Allen after replacing the receiver and told us very calmly as to not frighten us, "You will be taken immediately to the operating room. I need to perform an emergency Caesarean section. The ultrasound shows your babies are in distress, and I need to deliver them immediately."

I was lying down with an IV attached and probes on my stomach not clearly understanding the state of potential danger our babies are in. I look over at Allen whose eyes was watered, and he was looking pale.

The orderly entered my room, and I was scooted over onto the gurney. Allen followed along with me on route to the operating room. When we reached the attended destination, Allen reached for my hand and held it for a while as we gazed into each other's eyes exchanging no words. He let go of my hand, as I was being wheeled away from him into the operating room.

The room was very cold, which caused my body to shudder. Was I cold or nervous? Was it an involuntary response, my body reacting to the seriousness of my situation?

The OR nurses prepared my stomach for surgery and the anesthesiologist turned me over to my left side so he could administer the epidural. My body is still shaking; I cannot control it. The anesthesiologist does not seem concerned.

"The anesthesia has been administered," he announced as he assists me over onto my back. A sheet is placed in front of me to obscure my view. All I could see now is the anesthesiologist monitoring my vital signs.

Dr. Paul started to mark off the area on my stomach where he was going to cut. This is when I yelled out, "Dr. Paul, I can feel your hands!"

He immediately stopped what he was doing and turned to the anesthesiologist. "The epidural did not take. Do it again and get it right this time! These babies are in distress, and they need to be delivered immediately!"

After hearing the frustration in Dr. Paul's voice, I immediately began to be aware of my situation. The fog in my head had cleared, and I finally realized the urgency of my situation. I tried to control my shaking with the second attempt administering the epidural. Again it is administered, and I was rolled on my back. Dr. Paul again touched my stomach to see if I can feel anything, and I responded by saying no.

Because I was unable to see beyond a sheet propped up in front of my face, all I could hear were many different voices. I felt pressure on my stomach and a swooshing sound. The next thing I heard was Dr. Paul's voice announcing, "Here is baby number one." And then a minute later, "Here is baby number two."

Again, I heard more voices, shouting, "Suction please, set up the oxygen, and bring over the respirators." I felt like I was part of a hospital scene on a television show.

Most importantly, what I did not hear were my babies cry. Why were they not crying? Every movie or television show I watch delivering a baby, the baby always cries.

Dr. Paul finished stitching my stomach, approached me, touching my face tenderly in his compassionate way, and said, "You delivered twin boys. They are very tiny. I want to reassure you they are in excellent hands. There are two teams set up to care for each of your boys and they are extremely experienced caring for preemies." He took my hand, held it for a second, and then walked away.

I was carefully moved over to a gurney to be taken to the recovery room. At the doorway of the OR, I saw Allen. He was wearing hospital scrubs with his head and shoes covered as well. He took my hands and kissed me tenderly. "I just left them after following both teams upstairs to the Neonatal Intensive Care Unit [NICU] where they are being treated."

I stared at him with terror in my eyes, and he squeezed my hands as to comfort me. I immediately blurted out, "The first baby delivered, I want his name to be Michael and the second baby delivered, he will be Jason."

He shook his head in agreement and left me to return to the boys. We had four names picked out a few months previously so there will be no hesitation naming them when they are born.

I am still in the recovery room when one of the residents assigned to our boys stopped by to talk to me. He said, "Your boys are in very critical condition. They both are on respirators."

I stared at him in disbelief as he is talking. There were no words to say when one is confronted with this drastic situation. All I could feel or apprehend was my boys were very sick, very small and I was scared to death.

An hour later, while I was being wheeled toward the elevator to my assigned hospital room on the second floor, I was surprised to see my dad. He was looking for me.

"Allen called his parents and they called us just before you were taken to the operating room. All four of us rushed over to the hospital," he said.

As he was talking to me, I saw tears in his eyes. I never saw my father cry. His unexpected emotion caused my eyes to swell as well. In my anguished state, I cried out to my dad, "I didn't hear my boys cry! Why did they not cry?"

He held my hand and told me everything is going to be all right. The elevator door opened, I kissed him good-bye, and I was wheeled in. My thoughts are going in so many directions. I imagined a father's responsibility in this situation is to say this to a daughter. However, how was everything going to be all right if my boys were both on respirators, in the NICU and in critical condition?

First Week

The boys were in critical condition in the NICU supported by oxygen, respirators, and tubes surrounding their tiny bodies. Allen is allowed to enter the NICU to see the boys but our family and friends are unable to see them.

After arriving to my hospital room, I am unable to get out of bed. Allen brought me their pictures. "They are so tiny. How can I see anything clearly with all these tubes, wires, and respirators surround their little bodies, I can hardly see their faces," I said.

"Dear, I know it is upsetting looking at these pictures and not being able to see them. You will be able to see them real soon. I know they are tiny and it is frightening to look at them with all the tubes around their bodies. Please be patient and have confidence they will survive," he pleaded with me.

Allen alternated his visits periodically throughout the day sitting with me and the boys in NICU. The only connection to my boys is these pictures. I find myself staring at their pictures constantly.

The loving support from both my parents and in-laws are certainly appreciated as they visit throughout the day. The phone rings constantly from extended family and friends trying to comfort me. *It must be hard for them to call. What can one say during a time like this? I wouldn't know what to say to someone who just delivered twins, two months early, and in critical condition in the Intensive Care Nursery* were some wandering thoughts in my head throughout the day.

It was difficult to sleep in a hospital. I was constantly being awakened by a nurse who takes my vital signs through the night. My thoughts were, *Why am I in a single room? They probably don't want me exposed to moms whose babies are brought to them for feeding. I am the woman who has the critically ill twins in the nursery. I am sure they have good intentions, but I cannot help feeling segregated. It just continues to exasperate my situation.*

Allen arrived early in the morning after he experienced a difficult night sleeping as well. He walked into the hospital room, moved over to my bed, and kissed me. "How are you?"

My curt, somewhat brazen response was, "What would you expect from a woman who had major surgery yesterday, her twin boys are in severe condition, and I am feeling somewhat isolated?"

Allen gave me a questionable look and sat down on my bed, took my hand into his, and with no words spoken between us, we just used quiet time to contemplate and pray.

Before Allen came to my room, he saw the boys first. He said, "I have an update on the boys from their doctor. He told me, when they first arrived in the unit, their initial impression was Michael's condition appeared to be very critical."

He continued while I was staring into his eyes in fright, "Their initial assessment changed by this morning. Overnight, Michael's blood test shows an improvement in his blood oxygen level, and they removed his respirator successfully. Michael is breathing with the assistance of oxygen."

"Oh, how wonderful," I said. "How is Jason?"

Unfortunately, he continued, "Jason's blood studies reveal a very low blood oxygen level, and it is too dangerous to attempt removing the respirator at this time. His lungs are very weak due to his premature status."

Describing Jason as he did, with each word, caused my heart to skip a beat each howling description. *Oh my god*, I thought, *my poor baby.*

Allen left the hospital after sitting with me and seeing the boys throughout the day. He made one more stop, before heading home, to see the boys again.

Later on that evening the nurse on call rushed into my room to comfort me as she told me "Jason stopped breathing, and the CPR team has been called. His left lung collapsed, and it is necessary to perform a procedure to inflate the lung. I was just informed he is now stabilized." She continued to sit by my side while I called Allen. He returned to the hospital, and together, we, wait for further word on Jason.

After returning to the hospital and spending the remainder of the night with me, I pleaded with Allen to go home and get some rest. After he left, the nurse entered my room to bathe me and afterward, helped me out of the bed into a chair.

Later in the day, a nurse from NICU stopped in my room to talk with me. She pulled a chair close and sympathetically asked me, "Why haven't you visited your boys today?" She continued, "I will be happy to help you into a wheelchair and take you to see them. I will be with you the entire time answering any question you may have."

While trying not to be ungrateful, I reluctantly agreed, and she left my bedside to retrieve a wheelchair. My eyes began swelling with tears, and I am beginning to lose control of my emotions. I felt the need to talk to someone, so I called my sister Arlene. This is when the flood gate opened. For the first time since they were born, I am actually showing some emotion. My sister, being a wise woman, helped me to understand I am scared to see them. She told me she wished she could be with me but is unable to because she cannot leave my niece and nephew. However, she did encourage me to allow the nurse to take me to see the boys.

Before anyone can enter the NICU, the nurse explained, "It is crucial to thoroughly wash your hands and wear a sterile gown and hat on your head. The NICU needs to be germ-free, and these precautions are necessary in order to reassure complete sterilization of the unit."

We followed all the guidelines, and she wheeled me through the doors, and I am on my way to see the boys. "They are so tiny," I said as she pulled me up close to both of their incubators, which are next to each other.

She explained each tube and wire, which appears all tangled among each other across their tiny bodies. She encouraged me to hold their little hands. She helped me out of the wheelchair and placed me in a chair where I am situated between the two incubators, giving me better access to reach for their tiny hands.

"Holding their hands is crucial at this time to enhance their recovery. You and the boys need to bond. They will feel your presence," she said.

I sat in the chair between the two boys for an hour holding their hands and softly talking to them. The nurse returned and helped me back in my wheelchair, and I blew kisses to Michael and Jason as I left their room. My spirits are uplifted now that I found the courage to visit them. I called Allen to tell him I saw Michael and Jason for the first time. He was so happy for me and praised me for my courage. After ending our phone conversation, I thought about the events of today. *I crossed the hurdle from fear to deep love. They are my little angels. I will never allow myself to feel fear for them again. I need to be strong for both of them to recover.*

I was discharged a week after their birth without my little babies in my arms. There are no words to explain what it is like to leave the hospital after giving birth and having to leave them behind.

As part of my recovery, my doctor asked me to stay away from stairs for a week to allow my incision to heal and my stitches to stay secure. I live in a two-story house with one bathroom that is on the second level. I was forced to stay upstairs.

It was now one week after the boys were born on a Saturday night, and we had tickets for the Phillies baseball game. I encouraged Allen to go since he loves the Philadelphia Phillies, and I was thinking it will be good for him to get out. He left the house to pick up my brother-in-law Paul. My parents were over to keep me company.

It was 8:00 p.m., and the phone rang. I picked up the receiver. "Hello, yes, this is Mrs. Quate."

It is a doctor from NICU. "Jason is in serious distress and you and your husband should come immediately to the hospital."

I hang up the phone abruptly without saying anything.

"What happened?" Dad asked.

It took me a moment to absorb what he told me and answered, "Dad, Jason is in serious distress. I did not ask what happened. The doctor requested Allen and I to leave for the hospital as soon as possible. Oh my god, did he die? Maybe he didn't want to tell me on the phone."

Dad, trying to calm me down, asked, "Can you reach Allen at the stadium?"

"Yes," I exclaimed, "of course. I will call the stadium and give them our section number, row and seat, and they can find the usher stationed at our section."

I found the phone number and called. A very sympathetic woman apparently heard the anxiety in my voice responded, "Mrs. Quate, don't you worry, we will find your husband and give him the message." Surprisingly, ten minutes later the same woman called back to tell me my husband received the message and is on his way to the hospital.

I felt so helpless lying in bed. I wanted to dress and pleaded with Dad to take me to the hospital. However, dad refused to allow me to move. He told me to sit tight and wait for Allen's phone call.

It felt like hours have passed waiting for the phone to ring. Finally, Allen called and said, "Jason is now stable. He had a bleed that radiated to his brain. The doctor refers to this as an intraventricular hemorrhage. They successfully controlled it with emergency treatment."

After Mom and Dad left and Allen was on his way home, again my thoughts are all over the place. *Okay what does this mean? He could have died. I understand medical terminology and I understand how damaging a hemorrhage to the brain can be. It can cause brain damage. When one has a stroke and it bleeds into the brain, that person is a high risk for brain damage or death. It could also cause paralysis, depending on the section of the brain that is damaged. Did Jason develop brain damage?* I know these questions cannot be answered now. Only time will tell. We have to watch his progress. However, my heart is telling me Jason has a will to live. Within one week of birth, he had two major incidents that could have resulted in death. He did not die. This little angel of mine has a will to live for a reason I cannot comprehend now, but I have a feeling I will learn in the future.

Michael's Recovery

My routine is visiting Michael and Jason daily, sometimes twice in one day. Creating communication on a daily basis serves to be an important aspect in learning everything I can. This routine works well. I spend the day with the boys, and later, I sometimes return with Allen after dinner. The nurses continue to remind me to hold their tiny hands, talk to them, and cradle them in my arms. Hearing our voices and feeling our touch is something we can contribute to help in their recovery. It also contributes to bonding that is another important aspect to their recovery.

Holding Jason is definitely a challenge manipulating the ventilator and all the tubes surrounding him. The nurses are very supportive helping me hold Jason without the fear of disconnecting a vital life line.

Our personal life is on hold. We no longer have the ability or the strength to socialize with our friends. We have wonderful friends who are very supportive and will call us periodically to check in.

It is now one month since birth, and I have become acquainted with many of the nurses on all shifts, and they look forward to my visits.

Today, Michael has been transferred to the Transitional Unit, within NICU, considered a step up to full recovery. He is breathing room air and no longer needs the assistance of oxygen. The nurse asked me if I would like to feed him for the first time.

"Of course I will," I responded with joy. She placed him in my arms. He sucked on the nipple very willingly without any swallowing difficulties. How thrilled I was to hold this beautiful, tiny baby while he was sucking his nourishment. *This is what motherhood is all about*, I thought very happily.

I would often find a note on Michael's crib reminding the nurses his mom was coming to feed him. I would sit with him in a rocker in a room they assigned for mothers to feed their babies. I would hold his little hand, and he just would look right into my eyes. He now knew who I was. I was thrilled, and I looked forward to holding him and letting him feel the love flowing from my body to his tiny one.

Michael will be discharged when he reaches five pounds. Each day as I entered the NICU, I was obsessed with his weight chart. I was waiting anxiously for him to reach the milestone of five pounds so he can go home.

Unfortunately, Jason's condition had not changed. He was dependent on the respirator to breath for him and was unable to be weaned from it. Several doctors had been consulted, and they all agreed the longer Jason is dependent on the respiratory, his condition will continue to decline.

We clearly understood the dilemma. He was still breathing because of the respirator. Each day, he continued to be dependent on the respirator can lead to severe damage to his lungs. This was so critical because of the extreme pressure the respirator places on his very under-developed lungs. It could also cause another intraventricular hemorrhage, which will result in brain death.

Michael finally reached the desired weight of five pounds, and he was coming home. This placed us in a precarious position with mixed emotions. Our house was prepared for Michael's homecoming. Allen and I walked out of the hospital with Michael in my arms and with a heavy heart.

Michael was such a good baby. He quickly adapted to his new environment. We were now a family of three and we were praying to increase our family to four, hoping Jason will soon come home as well.

A few weeks later, after Michael was discharged, a doctor from NICU called and asked if Allen and I will come to the hospital; he would like to talk to us.

While standing around Jason's incubator, he carefully explained, "We attempted to wean Jason several times off the respirator unsuccessfully. His oxygen blood level drawn while he was off the respirator showed his lung capacity to be unstable. It was necessary to replace the respirator." He continued to explain sympathetically, "We are concerned, if Jason cannot be weaned from the respirator, it could prove to be fatal. The respirator is causing tremendous pressure on his lungs. We are watching him carefully but he is at risk to throw another blood clot. This one could prove to be fatal."

Back in the car and driving home, we began to consider the possibility of Jason's death. How are we going to deal with the death of our child? How are we were going to explain to Michael he had a twin brother who died. The possibility of Jason's passing was in both of our thoughts, but this is the first time we actually communicated our feelings outwardly.

A few weeks after the meeting with the doctor, we were both preparing to start our day. The phone rang. I answered it, wondering who could be calling this early. "Hello?"

"Mrs. Quate, I am the nurse assigned to Jason in NICU today, and the doctor on call asked me to call you. He would like both of you to come to the hospital as soon as you can."

I called my mother-in-law and asked if she could watch Michael. Mom arrived within ten minutes, and Allen and I both left for the hospital. We are both very quiet in the car. I know I am feeling very anxious. Allen is quietly driving not saying a word. We both are wondering if Jason died.

As we anxiously approached Jason's bedside, we found him lying quietly and the familiar tube that had been in his mouth since birth is no longer present.

"Where is the respirator?" I asked with a look of surprise and wonderment. I quickly looked at the monitor and was very grateful to see the lines moving up and down. I am aware of the familiar beeps I became accustomed hearing in the past three months. Jason's vital signs are definitely apparent on the monitor.

The doctor quickly approached after seeing the perplexing look on both of our faces. He explained, "Apparently, some time during the night, Jason, from what we can only determine, pulled a wire connected to the respirator that caused it to disconnect." He continued seeing we were getting anxious. "The nurses were not aware of what occurred because the alarm, which would automatically signal a distress call, did not go off. They found Jason breathing without any distress, and his vital signs were stable. We took a blood sample immediately and his blood oxygen level was in a normal range."

Allen and I looked at each other and began hugging and crying as the nurse and doctor watched with joy. It occurred to me, remembering we were talking about his fate, Jason heard us talking, and this little angel is not ready to die. He has a purpose in life, and he will achieve it. He is one of God's angels for sure.

Jason's Discharge

Jason was off the respirator, and his vital signs and blood oxygen levels were improving. The hospital staff was preparing him for discharge.

I entered the NICU to visit Jason. He has been transferred to the Transitional Unit. I picked him up and took him over to the rocking chair in the lounge when I noticed his skin and nail beds are turning blue. "What is happening to him!" I yelled.

The nurse quickly ran over and took his vital signs while I was still holding him. The doctor arrived a few minutes later. After a few minutes, Jason's color returned to normal. I started feeding his bottle as the doctor explained to me what happened.

"Mrs. Quate, Jason is experiencing apnea spells at least once or twice daily. This is not uncommon for a preemie experiencing trauma similar to Jason's history," he said.

"What can we do to stop this?" I asked frantically. "Will this stop?"

He sat down by my side in an attempt to comfort me. "We do not know the answer to your question. Like I said, this is typical for a preemie like Jason. Only time will tell. We are monitoring the episodes to chart how often they occur. According to his chart, it shows they are slowing down. We are waiting for the episodes to slow to at least once a day in order to prepare him for discharge."

That evening, while sitting around the table eating dinner, I told Allen what occurred while visiting Jason.

"Is this all he said to you?" he asked.

"They are waiting for the episodes to slow down so they can discharge him!" I responded questionably.

"Slow down," Allen responded. "What does that mean?"

It didn't make any sense to either one of us.

I visited Jason every day the following week. I continued to observe Jason's episodes of apnea. I watched carefully to try to learn and understand. I was not scared because I know there were nurses and doctors around to call, if I need help. I witnessed a few episodes, similar to the first one I saw, he stops breathing, turns blue, and faints. This will startle him to begin breathing again. His color would return to normal, and he would look up at me as he opens his eyes. It appears these episodes make him very tired, and he will suddenly fall asleep.

I knew the doctor will discharge him soon, so I made it a point to observe him closely when he had an episode. It was quite possible I will be alone with him at home when he will have an episode, and I wondered if I am prepared for this. I was ashamed to admit I was scared. I am not a nurse. I was frightened beyond belief and emotionally drained.

Unknown and Inexperience

Jason was discharged in February of 1980, four months after birth. The day we walked out with Jason in my arms, I was handed a piece of paper that consisted of an appointment to take Jason to the clinic for a follow-up visit one week later.

The evening of Jason's homecoming, Allen left to attend a class at Drexel University. He is taking classes to earn a degree in Electrical Engineering. He didn't want to leave me alone with the boys the first night after Jason came home but I urged him to go. My reasoning is I needed to develop a routine so I might as well start immediately. Oh my, I am pretending to be a brave mom but am I really?

It was feeding time, and I was sitting on the sofa with Michael on one side of me and Jason on the other in their infant seats with two bottles in my hands. It occurred to me I should feed Michael first. I was familiar with Michael. He drinks his milk easily and quickly. I picked up Michael and started feeding him. Just a few minutes later, Jason started to cry. I did not panic and decided to continue feeding Michael. I was watching Jason and he appeared to be holding his breath. His skin was turning blue along with his nail beds.

I immediately placed Michael back in his seat and grabbed Jason and held him. I started to cry. I didn't know what to do since

I wasn't given advice from the doctors when he was discharged. I started walking around the room, crying and praying he will start breathing again. Finally, he jerks as I was holding him. I looked at his face and his eyes appeared to roll back in its sockets and he immediately began to breathe again with his skin color returning to normal. Jason was exhausted in my arms and Michael is crying because he wanted more milk.

I was in a state of hysteria. I sat down after placing Jason in his cradle. *Now what do I do?* I thought. *I am so confused. Why did they discharge him? There is something wrong with him, and I cannot deal with it. Allen is not home all day. What am I going to do?*

I knew I needed someone with me, I was so scared. I picked up the phone and called my mother-in-law, and she came running over along with Allen's dad. Mom saw the state I was in and picked Michael up and continued to feed him and then prepared him for bed. I picked up Jason, managed to wake him and fed him without further incident.

With mom's help I finally calmed down. Both boys fell asleep, and Mom and Dad stayed with me to keep me company and we waited until Allen returned home. Allen's mom urged us to call the hospital the next day and ask for him to be readmitted. I felt helpless as a mother having to return my baby to the hospital. It would appear I didn't want him. I certainly didn't want to feel this way.

"You are making the right decision," Mom reassured. "He should never have been discharged today. It is obvious he needs further evaluation and you two need to request a second opinion," Mom continues, finally speaking her mind. We need to listen to both of them. They raised two children with their own trial and tribulations and we needed to listen to their advice.

The next day, I called the Neonatal Intensive Care Unit and they advised us to bring Jason to the emergency ward. He was admitted to the pediatric unit.

It is very clear to both Allen and I the doctors in this hospital did not know what to do for Jason. Our parents encouraged us to request a second opinion, and we agreed. We had Jason transferred to the St Christopher's Hospital for Children, and he was placed under the care of a pediatric neurologist, Dr. Lawrence Brown.

With Jason in an ambulance, we followed him to St. Christopher's Hospital. Upon arrival, we were both very impressed with their quality of care, both the doctors and nurses. They were very attentive to our needs and sympathetic as well. We immediately liked Dr. Brown with his comforting ways and how he explained all the procedures he planned out for Jason as part of his evaluation. He ordered several tests including EEG, ultrasound of his brain, and a barium swallow to rule out a reflux.

The barium swallow test is a medical imaging procedure used to examine the upper GI tract, which includes the esophagus and the stomach. Barium sulfate is the medium they use with this test. The patient swallows the barium sulfate as it coats the esophagus. This enables the hollow structure to be imaged. The test was performed in the radiology department. I waited for Jason in his room.

I was sitting in his room reading a book when I heard over the speaker a stat call. I knew what stat meant. They were calling for the cardiac resuscitation team. What created my panic state was they were calling the team for the radiology department. I quickly ran to the nurse station in a panic and asked the nurse at the desk, "Is this call for Jason? Do you know?"

"Yes, Mrs. Quate, we just received a phone call. Dr. Brown will be up to talk to you soon."

I returned to Jason's room shaking all over. I immediately called Allen at work and he left for the hospital. As I am waiting in Jason's room shocked and anxious for some news, the nurse approached me. "Mrs. Quate, Dr. Brown just called and asked me to take you to the intensive care unit. Jason has been transferred there after they stabilized him. Dr. Brown will explain everything when you arrive."

When I arrived at the intensive care unit, I am escorted to Jason's bed and found him on a respirator. I looked at Dr. Brown and the tears started to flow. He guided me out of the room and sat down with me to explain, "Jason aspirated the barium. It appears the aspiration caused aspirating pneumonia, and it was necessary to place him on the respirator. He stopped breathing that necessitated calling the stat team to revive him. I requested a consultation with a pulmonary specialist." A few minutes later, Allen arrived, and Dr. Brown repeated what he told me.

Jason's condition started to improve and the respirator was removed without incident. He was transferred back to a hospital room a few days later.

I was extremely blessed to have both my mother-in-law and our neighbor Jacqueline who babysat for Michael so I could be with Jason every day.

One day, while sitting with Jason, I received a phone call from the business office asking me to stop by their office some time that day. After arriving and sitting down at the woman's desk she explained to me Jason exceeded his health insurance coverage when he was discharged from Albert Einstein Medical Center. However, she proceeded to say, "We called your health insurance company, and they informed me Jason should be eligible for catastrophic coverage. I applied, and Jason was accepted."

After returning to Jason's room, it finally occurred to me they rushed Jason's discharge at Albert Einstein Hospital because his insurance was running out. If he exceeded the insurance coverage, why didn't they tell us? This definitely was a learning experience, and now, I wondered what I have in store for me in years to come. How will I ever manage to sift through the bureaucracy of red tape? I certainly have a lot to learn.

Twenty-three days later, our dear Jason was discharged again. However, this time, Dr. Brown prepared us. Jason was given a diagnosis that explains his apnea spells. He has respiratory distress syndrome that is common in preemies with premature lungs and the long-term effects of dependency on the respirator. The day of discharge, we walked out of the hospital with Jason and an apnea monitor.

In my opinion, the monitor was a gift from heaven and a gift from Dr. Brown. I placed Jason on the monitor 24/7. Keeping Jason on the monitor gave me the peace of mind I needed. Knowing it would alert me when Jason has an apnea spell was so reassuring. Knowing why he is having these spells made a boat load of difference in my mind. I was now aware of why it happened, and I was reassured he will come out of it breathing again.

Jason's personality was starting to emerge. He was beginning to look around at his surroundings. He started recognizing who I am. When I fed him, he looked lovingly into my eyes, and my heart started to flutter. We were bonding. He is no longer the stranger I saw just one month earlier. It appeared to me he recognized his mom and was starting to show a sense of belonging and being loved. It was a new beginning.

Challenges to Overcome

We were starting to slowly adjust to a routine of daily living as a family of four. The monitor was sensitive and beeped with any slight movement. With the cradle in the living room where Jason can be seen, his skin color was pink, and he was not in distress when the monitor beeped. He started watching Michael play. He was beginning to watch television and he appeared to listen to our conversations. He was beginning to respond with a smile. His eyes were alert, and he followed our movements throughout the house. He was either in his infant seat or lying on his stomach when sleeping, but always on the monitor. He needed to sit upright for at least a half hour after feeding so he could digest his formula and avoid the risk of aspirating. I was able to perform my daily chores and played with Michael while Jason was in his cradle either sleeping or watching us.

We had another cradle in our bedroom at the front of our bed. When Jason finished his evening feeding, I would place him back in his infant seat on the monitor. When I heard him moaning, I would take him out of the infant seat, laid him down on the monitor on his stomach to sleep. This process was repeated when he woke for his next feeding. With all the moving around during the night, listening for every breath he took, the monitor going off with every slight movement, and having to check if Jason was okay, a good night's sleep was just not going to happen. Jason's welfare was my number one concern.

Jason began vomiting his formula one month after returning home from St. Christopher's Hospital. I took him to see Dr. Brown.

"When we performed the barium swallow before he aspirated, the technician detected a swallowing issue. She also noted in her report he had a reflux that places him at a high risk for aspiration. However, at that time, I decided to wait and see how Jason adjusts during the remainder of his hospitalization. He was sucking the nipple without difficulty at the time of discharge. I felt there were no repercussions with the reflux, and I didn't see a need to explore the issue further," he said.

He continued, "He has some muscle rigidity throughout his body. His vomiting could also be caused by a lack of muscle control. I am recommending we start tube feeding. I do not think this will be a permanent situation since I believe Jason will eventually gain control of his reflux and with therapy, range of motion will help. It will also improve as he gains more weight. As he gets stronger, he will have better control of his muscles."

After hearing words such as *muscle rigidity*, *reflux*, *therapy*, and *range of motion*, it should have prompted me to ask why was he rigid and why did he not have control?

Before I left Dr. Brown's office, the nurse came in and taught me how to place the tube in Jason's nose, down through his throat, into his esophagus. She showed me how to use a stethoscope to listen for a bubbling sound in his stomach that will indicate the tube is placed properly.

I left the office feeling overwhelmed. Can I do this? However, I somehow knew I can do anything I needed to for Jason.

A visiting nurse arrived the next day to monitor my progress and to teach Allen how to tube feed Jason as well. "You both are doing very well. You learn very quickly," she told us. Her words were reassuring.

A few months after initiating the tube feeding, I took Jason for a routine visit with Dr. Brown. He suggested we try introducing feeding by mouth again once a day to see if he was able to keep the feedings down.

It was successful, and he swallowed without difficulty and kept the formula down with each attempt. Eventually, the tube feeding was discontinued.

Now that we solved one issue another began. Jason was having trouble with mucus building up in his chest. He started coughing up mucus. Again, I took Jason to see Dr. Brown. He reminded me, "Jason has respiratory distress syndrome, and his lungs are weak. He appears he is having difficulty with excess mucus along with his lung disease and rigidity making it difficult for him to cough. With the reflux, he cannot control his coughing and swallowing causing him to cough up his mucus." To sum it up, he reminded me again he had a high risk for aspirating. He recommended attempting suctioning out his mucus when it appeared he was losing control. Again a visiting nurse visited our house with a suction machine and showed both Allen and I how to suction the mucus from Jason's esophagus and throat.

Our dear Jason is developing a sweet personality with a beautiful big smile. He doesn't cry often. He cries only when he isn't feeling well, more like a moan. He also developed a defined pout to let me know he was in pain and would moan and pout when he wanted to communicate his feelings.

I began to learn how to distinguish his cries. I am now familiar with his "angry" cry. His "angry" cry presented itself when he appears to be out of control. This is when he lost his breath, turned blue, and passed out. Now I was wise to his behavior. I did not pick him up in a panic when he started holding his breath with his "angry" cry. I became much calmer. The fog was clearing, and I was beginning to see Jason in a different light. I now saw him as a "special needs child." I used this term sparingly because I didn't really know what it encapsulates. What I did know, he was different than Michael, and I began to understand there was something wrong with him.

I started to observe him more closely when he had his "angry" cry episodes. He would start by holding his breath. It appeared he held his cry for an unusual long period. He would reach a point where he would be unable to catch his breath, and this is when he turned blue and passed out. You need to understand I was basing this only on my observation of Jason and my "mother instincts," which were beginning to come alive. I was not a doctor. I was forming my own opinion. I believed he knew what he was doing. He was a very good child, but when he tried to get my attention, he knew what to do to get it by crying hard that caused his apnea spells. When I finally figured out what he was doing, I stopped giving him the attention he wanted. Eventually, his "angry cry" stopped and so did the apnea spells. I believed I solved that problem. I had no doubt this is what he was doing all along. If I had to go through the five-month ordeal Jason experienced, I probably would have done the same thing out of frustration.

He finally did stop using his apnea spells to gain attention, but it didn't stop altogether. One night, Jason demonstrated for his Poppy (Allen's dad) how he was able to hold his breath. We were suctioning mucus, and Jason did not like this procedure. So, since his Poppy was watching, he thought he would demonstrate what he was able to do! However, he didn't return his breath quickly enough, and we all started to panic. Allen called the paramedics. I held Jason to my chest, and he finally jerked and started breathing again. Poppy completely turned white with fright. The funny part of this story was when the paramedics arrived, Jason was sitting on my lap and he smiled with delight because the excitement they presented. Michael was sitting on the floor staring at them. He had a look of excitement as well because firemen were in our house. Jason clearly entertained Michael with his antics.

When the boys were eight months old I took them for a routine pediatric appointment. Our doctor recommended Jason be enrolled in an early intervention program. Fortunately, I knew what early intervention was all about because my niece attended an early intervention program for developmental delays. I contacted the program my niece attended and scheduled an appointment for an evaluation.

The day of the appointment, Jason saw the physical therapist first and then the occupational therapist. When the evaluation was completed, we all sat down to discuss their plan of action for Jason. After the meeting, I talked with the social worker to start the paper work associated with gathering medical history, family history, and so on. As she was filling out the application, she started verbalizing what she was writing and said, "I see Jason's diagnosis is cerebral palsy." I did not respond and sat quietly while she finished the paperwork. She explained, "Jason will be placed in the half day program, and he will receive physical, occupational and speech therapy. The attention will be focused on constant range of motion to keep his muscles relaxed." It sounded pretty wonderful with a good planned out program. However, I was preoccupied, still thinking about what she said previously— cerebral palsy!

As soon as I was able to I visited the library and researched cerebral palsy associated with premature babies. I read in the books I found, preemies that had a brain hemorrhage like Jason were a high risk for cerebral palsy. I also read there were several different types of cerebral palsy. However, I stopped my research at that point because I didn't want or need to know anymore. I was already overloaded dealing with the diagnosis of cerebral palsy.

At our next appointment with Dr. Brown, I abruptly asked, "Does Jason have cerebral palsy?"

"Jason does have cerebral palsy, but it isn't my practice to label a child so young," he responded.

I looked somewhat frustrated and responded, "I respect your honesty and your hesitation labeling a child, but I clearly need you to know; I need a diagnosis in order to help my son. I am his mother and how can I help my son and get him the services he needs without an honest approach to his condition."

The approach I took responding to Dr. Brown proved to be the beginning of my new role as Jason's advocate and the beginning of a great relationship with Dr. Brown. There were no limits to our communications after I spoke my peace. He now understood he was dealing with one tough mother. After this visit, I finally realized I will never again be the shy, introverted person I was before my boys were born.

Jason started Ken Crest Early Intervention Program in 1980, eight months after discharge from St. Christopher's Hospital. He was scheduled to attend a five-day program from 9:00 a.m. to 12:00 nn. Michael and I took Jason on his first day. I laid Jason down on the mat on the floor and then looked up. At the same time, a young mother laid her daughter down on the mat next to Jason and also looked up. We saw each other and said hello. This was the first time Nancy and I met. Nancy's young child, Abby, was starting her first day as well and had the same schedule as Jason. Meeting Nancy this first day was the beginning of a long-term friendship through the years, and we became very good friends with a close bond. We supported each other through the years, and a true friendship has been born.

Early Intervention

Jason and Michael celebrated their second birthday in grand style. Jason was still attending Ken Crest. Our lives were routine, hectic, and structured. Our days began saying good-bye to Daddy as he left for work each day. My days began by getting both boys washed, dressed, and downstairs for their breakfast. With all of the above accomplished, we leave for Ken Crest, and then Michael and I have an opportunity to spend some quality time together.

We picked Jason up each afternoon and drive home. Normally, this would be a routine chore for most households but not ours. Getting Michael and Jason up and out into the car alone was a big accomplishment, especially in the winter when leggings and heavy winter coats are necessary. It never failed; after I get them all snuggled and warm, I would bend down to pick up Jason and detect a familiar odor. Oh yes, Jason did it again. Jason would always poop at the most inconvenient times. Michael wasn't an angel either; there were times when he would do the same, even the same time as Jason. I wonder if they were working on a conspiracy tactic to see how much Mommy can handle. They actually enjoyed watching me work so hard. I am now addressing my readers who are moms. I know you are laughing now because it happens to you as well!

They are seventeen months old, and Michael was still not walking independently. He walked around the living room holding onto furniture, but he would not let go to walk freely on his own. Because Michael wasn't walking yet, I would have a problem transporting Jason to and from Ken Crest. I needed to support Jason so he would not jerk back. Therefore, I would hold him on my hip with his back against my chest and my arms under him so I would have a good grip on him. Remember, Michael was not walking independently, and I could not leave Michael in the car while I took Jason into the school. Picture this, I am was holding Jason as described and was dragging Michael along, forcing him to walk with me as he was crying because he wanted to be held as well. Okay, Moms, are you still relating!

Lunch in our household with just me was certainly not a typical lunch time affair. Michael would not always cooperate. Both boys were now eating baby food. You would think it would be easy as opening a jar and feeding them. If you could only see me trying to feed both of them at lunch, you would crack up laughing.

I would like to lay out a scenario if I may. It was pretty funny, and if I had a video camera, I would have sent the video to *America's Funniest Home Videos* and probably would have earned a lot of money. As you know, Jason was having difficulty with swallowing. He coughed a lot and many times I found myself splattered with food all over my chest and face. Jason looked at me and laughed. Michael watched the scene and thought it was funny and started to spit his food out of his mouth aiming for me as well. It was definitely a three ring circus every meal at the Quate residence.

Jason graduated from his cradle in front of our bed and was now sharing a bedroom with Michael. Apparently, they loved being in the same room together, especially Michael. He enjoyed having his brother with him so he can be entertained. Jason made sounds, lifted his head off the mattress, and looked up at Michael, and they both would crack up.

Michael must have been a heavy sleeper because Jason snored very loudly. I believe you could hear him snoring through the walls of our house. However, I never received any complaints from our neighbors.

Entering their room in the morning or after a nap, you needed a gas mask. A most delightful pungent odor approached me as I entered their room. They both had stinky diapers to change, oh my!

I have to admit I was blessed with two boys who liked to sleep. They were always ready for their nap after lunch, around one, and they would sleep for three hours every day. I was very grateful. I now had time to relax. I would either watch television, do needlepoint, or if the weather was nice, I would go outside and chat with the neighbors.

We lived in a row home and our neighbors, who shared our outside stoop, had a big old tree on their lawn. On a hot day, we would sit under the tree, which provided shade. It was actually a few degrees cooler under this tree. After the boys woke up from their nap I would take them outside and place them under the big tree with us. I brought out the playpen where I laid Jason, and Pepper, the neighbor's dog, laid down right next to the playpen. This dog believed it was her duty to protect Jason. What a great dog she was!

The Wendeler's—Jacqueline, Karl, Paula, and Michael—were the best neighbors anyone could wish for. Michael and Jason loved Jacqueline and Paula. When Jason had an appointment, Jacqueline or Paula would watch Michael. Both of them would also watch Jason if I needed to take Michael somewhere. We also had other very special babysitters who were good friends of Paula. Lisa and Maureen were the greatest young girls and loved my children unconditionally. I always knew I had someone to call if I needed a babysitter.

I have another funny story to share. It involved Jason, Jacqueline, and my sister Arlene. My sister offered to watch Jason for me one day when I needed to take Michael somewhere. Arlene never experienced Jason's breath holding. Apparently, Jason wasn't happy because I didn't take him with me. I suppose he felt this was a good time to try out his "crying trick" with Aunt Arlene. He started crying hard, held his breath, and turned blue. I was told Arlene grabbed Jason and ran into Jacqueline's house screaming for help. Without being too technical, let me just say Jacqueline was indisposed at the time. When she was free, Jacqueline ran down the stairs, called the paramedics, and by the time they arrived Jason already fainted, recovered, and was sitting on Arlene's lap looking at the paramedics as if to say, "What are you doing here? I was just playing around with my aunt Arlene. I wanted to show her what I could do!" I do not believe Arlene volunteered to babysit again.

Nancy's child Abby was two weeks older then the boys. Ken Crest had a very active parents' support group and both Allen and I and Nancy and Nancy's husband Mark participated in their functions. Nancy's husband Mark was the president of the group, and I was the vice president. The main purpose of the group, besides providing support, was fundraising. We had one main fundraiser a year that was "A Night at the Races." It was a very successful fundraiser, and we earned a lot of money for Ken Crest.

Nancy took Abbey to see Dr. Brown. We both found Dr. Kubacki, an ophthalmologist/surgeon for our children as well. I considered myself extremely privileged to find a great eye doctor. Dr. Kubacki's practice was in St. Christopher's Hospital. Jason had crossed eyes caused by his muscle tightness around his eyes. When I first took Jason to see Dr. Kubacki, he told me it may take a few surgeries to correct Jason's eyes due to his spasticity. He also said it was his experience the eyes tend to return back to its normal position which would require more than one surgery to finally correct them. However, after Jason's first surgery and returning to his office two months later, Jason's eyes did not revert back. Dr. Kubacki was surprised but pleased, and I left impressed with this surgeon.

I received update reports related to Jason's progress from Ken Crest. Jason always would come home with copies of reports and notes from the therapists. During my quiet times, I would sit and read everything so I could keep up with Jason's progress. I filed everything away so I could refer to them later if needed.

One day while I was sitting quietly and reading a report, a new diagnosis quickly popped out and took me by surprise. It appeared Jason now was referred to have "spastic quadriplegic cerebral palsy." With my knowledge of medical terminology, I knew what this meant. Medical terms consist of prefixes and suffixes and they all have their individual definitions. If you separate the above with the prefixes and suffixes, it translates to be an individual who has a condition of cerebral palsy involving all four limbs. The muscles in all four limbs are tight in nature, translation, spastic. This is considered a severe form of cerebral palsy. When all four limbs are affected, it more than likely it includes the entire body. In Jason's case, it appeared it had because he already was having difficulty with swallowing, which meant his chest muscles were affected. Jason's neck was also affected because he was having difficulty keeping his neck and back in line with his spine for him to sit up straight in his chair. We used pillows to try and keep his head in line but his tightness always fought the adjustment.

One afternoon, while Michael and I were picking up Jason from Ken Crest, the social worker stopped me on my way out and asked if I would please join her in her office.

All three of us entered her office and sat at her desk. Now I am concerned as to what was on her mind. She begins to say, "I was approached by the occupational therapist earlier this week. She apparently has been observing Michael for a few weeks. I don't want to frighten you, Mrs. Quate, but she feels Michael should be evaluated."

"Why? What is her justification? She only sees him occasionally. How can she come to a conclusion without obvious cause?" I asked.

She moved over to sit directly across from me and held my hand in the attempt to calm me down and continued, "Mrs. Quate, it was her professional opinion based on her experience as well. She knows the psychological levels a child of Michael's age should be at and it was her opinion, just by observation, Michael appeared to be behind. We all are aware of their birth history. Michael was a preemie and did have some oxygen deprivation at birth. She feels, based on his history, this justifies her to rule out any potential problems."

I have to say I was at first shocked, but after giving it some thought throughout the rest of the afternoon, I began to realize her recommendation was valid. I must admit I was scared. I do not want or need to hear Michael is delayed.

Allen and I talked it over and we both agreed it would be to our benefit and Michael's for him to be evaluated. However, we are both scared to hear the results. How much more can we handle? Are we strong enough to care for two children with problems?

Thankfully, the psychologist who evaluates the children at Ken Crest was willing to evaluate Michael. An appointment was scheduled for the following week I was in the room with Michael while she went through pertinent psychological testing with him.

A week after the evaluation, Allen and I scheduled an appointment to discuss the results of the tests. We were told Michael had mild motor and fine motor delays. The psychologist strongly recommended we contact Easter Seals and make an appointment for Michael for more intense evaluation. She also suggested they have a wonderful therapy program that could suit Michael's needs.

Jason received limited physical therapy at Ken Crest. We decided to make an appointment for both boys to be evaluated at Easter Seals. If I was going to take Michael weekly, I might as well take Jason along. Jason will definitely benefit from additional physical therapy.

I called Easter Seals and scheduled an appointment for Michael and Jason. The therapist assigned to evaluate Jason received, prior to our visit, a report from Ken Crest to help her understand Jason's complex problems. She also called me to ask additional questions before the visit.

We arrived at Easter Seals, and they asked me to wait in the lobby while the boys were being evaluated. When both evaluations were completed, the boys were brought out to me. The occupational therapist agreed with the prior evaluation from Ken Crest and suggested a plan of action for Michael. I agreed to Michael getting one-hour therapy session once per week. She assured me I was making the right decision because the earlier we start therapy with Michael, the more chance we will see improvement. She was very compassionate and made me feel at ease.

The physical therapist approached me and praised me for the decision to increase Jason's physical therapy treatments.

"The more range of motion Jason receives can certainly be beneficial for his well being," she said.

I am feeling more comfortable now that Allen and I made the decision. I now am reassured we are doing everything we can to help both of our boys.

We were getting ready to leave when the physical therapist stopped me at the door. She appeared to be anxious and this made me feel anxious as well.

What is wrong? I thought.

She hesitated and then said, "Mrs. Quate, when we talked on the phone and you described Jason to me I have to be honest with you, I was extremely nervous to meet Jason. I never worked with a child with Jason's disabilities and didn't know what to expect. I was anticipating he will be difficult to work with, crying and fighting with me as I move his muscles. However, today when I met him, he smiled at me, it just blew me away. I then realized I am with a unique child. I did not expect a child with his severe problems to be so cooperative, especially at his age. He did not cry with any of my range of motion movements. Most children with Jason's condition would fuss and be uncooperative. I was thrilled when I finished my evaluation; Jason looked at me with the sweetest smile. I absolutely love your child. He is a unique little boy, and I am looking forward to spending time with him."

I walked out of the building with the biggest grin on my face. I am thinking to myself as I guided both boys into the van and we left for home, *Thank you for being such an angel, little Jason. Your pleasant personality will help you in the future in ways I can only imagine, but I believe it will suit you well.*

Jason knew a smile would get him everything he wanted. He knew that if he smiled, he would get positive attention. He now was an expert at smiling, especially at pretty women. He definitely was a flirter, and everyone who had contact with him knew it and they loved his flirting.

Our daily routine continued with mornings at Ken Crest one afternoon a week at Easter Seals. Nancy and I started looking into another early intervention program that would provide a full day program and transportation. We found United Cerebral Palsy Association (UCPA) which had a program suitable for both of our needs and criteria, and we enrolled our children. The new program would provide more time with Michael. The definite plus with this program was the transportation they provided.

Vacations and Daily Living

Michael started nursery school at the local Synagogue, and Jason began attending United Cerebral Palsy Early Intervention Program five days a week. The bus picked Jason up at eight and dropped him off around four. It was the first time I had a chance to spend quiet time alone. I listened to music and cleaned the house. I did some reading, needlepoint, or even spent quality time with good friends. I didn't realize how stressed out I was now that I found the time for myself to relax.

My parents retired several years ago, and purchased a condominium in Florida. They spend half the year in Philadelphia and the other half in Florida. Floridian's use the term "snow birds" that describes northerners who escape from the cold and snow of the northern winters to the warmth of sunny Florida. They enjoyed their life in Florida. They had many friends and participated in social activities keeping them active.

It was time to take a vacation, and we decided to fly down to Florida to visit my parents and we took the boys with us. We know it will be hectic with the boys, but we wanted them to see their grandparents.

Jason was now in a specialized stroller, and we embarked the plane first to allow us time to get situated. Jason's stroller needed to be stored in the baggage compartment. When you travel with twins at this age and especially with a special needs child, you need to plan ahead; otherwise, the plane trip can go bad really quickly. For this reason, we fed them both before boarding the plane. Our flight was scheduled during the lunch hour, so we were offered lunch on board. Neither one of us expected to eat since we were holding the boys on our laps. We were pleasantly surprised when the nice gentleman who was sitting across from us, offered to hold Michael for Allen so he could enjoy his lunch. After Allen ate, I gave Jason to him and I ate something.

After the food issue was resolved, Michael began to get restless and wanted to wander around the plane holding onto anything he could to balance himself; including the chess board a couple had laid across their laps. Michael managed to swipe his hands across the board and all the chess pieces fell to the floor. Oh my, what can you say but "So sorry!"

We finally arrived. My parents were prepared for our visit and rented baby furniture.

We occupied the boys with playing in the pool, taking long walks, and enjoying the special open-air bus the residents use to take to and from their home to the Club House. It stopped at every corner to pick up and drop off people. Michael and Jason were having so much fun riding in this bus. However, it appeared the residents weren't as pleased to see us even when Jason flirted with them. I tried to evaluate why they appeared displeased. Did they not want our intrusion on their bus, or did they feel uncomfortable with Jason's presence? I was aware of Jason being stared at and it made me realize what our future will present with people staring at our sweet child.

With Jason getting older and somewhat more difficult to care for, he appeared reluctant to travel. Planning our second trip to Florida, we decided to drive. This trip proved to be far from pleasant compared to our first trip. Jason was now in a wheelchair. Having to remove everything in the trunk to reach for Jason's wheelchair was an effort. We needed access to his wheelchair at least a few times a day stopping for meals and at night at the motel. We finally arrived at my parent's house, and both Allen and I were already exhausted.

Jason cried through the first night. Jason did not typically cry for any reason other than indicating he was not feeling well. I smelled his ears and I immediately knew he had an ear infection, probably in both ears. I knew he needed amoxicillin (antibiotic). However, a doctor needed to give me a prescription. I called several pediatricians, and they all refused to see Jason after I described his condition. I was so frustrated; I only wanted my baby to feel better. We decided to take him to the nearest hospital's emergency room. The doctor walked into the room, and I proceeded to tell him, "My son has an ear infection, probably both ears, and he needs Amoxicillin."

After a routine exam including vital signs, he finally looks into both ears and tells me, "Mrs. Quate, you are correct, your son has bilateral ear infections." He hands me the script and we walked out of the room, heading home with one stop at the pharmacy to fill the prescription. We doubled the dose for the first day, and Jason responded well and slept through the night.

The remaining visit with my parents was pleasant and uneventful. We headed home. During the long drive home, we discussed the vacation and reached the conclusion this probably will be the last vacation for Jason. It was apparently clear Jason was not happy in unfamiliar surroundings. He tolerated the week but we knew he was making the best of an uncomfortable situation. He didn't have his normal happy personality he was known for.

We continued to take Jason on day trips to the Jersey shore. Jason will tolerate any change of unfamiliarity the best he can because he was a good child. He tolerated the beach by lying on a blanket with an umbrella and a towel on him for added protection from the sun. Interestingly, he never cried or acted out. He just does not like being away from familiar surroundings, and we eventually understood and stopped taking him on day trips as well, especially the beach. This was difficult for us to accept because we wanted him to take part in our family activities such as trips to the park, going to the shore, going to the playground, and an amusement park. However, he was much happier staying home with Bubby and Poppy. As he grew older, we realized he was going through an uncomfortable adjustment phase. It is important to mention Jason did love to go places. He especially loved the mall. The colors surrounding him and all the people he passed at the mall were very stimulating, and he enjoyed this kind of day trip.

When the boys turned three, it became clear Michael was taller than Jason. Michael looked more like Jason's older brother. Jason's legs were "frog-like" in appearance probably due to the beginning of atrophy because of muscle deterioration from lack of mobility. He didn't have head control and he was unable to sit up without support.

As Jason's mother, I still see Jason as my baby. I chose to ignore the differences in their appearance. I was not facing reality. Honestly, I didn't really know what I was feeling. At times, I would pick Jason up, show him to my family or friends, and ask, "Does Jason look disabled?" Wasn't this crazy? It appeared my mind was playing games with me.

I ignored the inadequacies in my obviously demented mind and requested an opinion with an endocrinologist. He examined Jason and suggested to admit him to the hospital for an overnight stay for a few tests to see if he had a thyroid deficiency. All the tests proved to be negative.

Thinking back, after so many years, it appears all of Jason's doctors were appeasing my state of mind and not sharing their true opinions. Perhaps they really didn't know themselves and just went along with my suggestions hoping to find an answer as well.

We tried very hard to create a normal family atmosphere. Allen would play with the boys like a daddy normally would, tackling with them and roughly rolling around the floor. Jason loved everything about playtime. Allen would take turns lightly throwing each one on the couch, and when it was Jason's turn, Jason would cry and kick his legs and move his arms with the anticipation of excitement. He loved playtime and never would show any signs of being scared. The rougher Allen was with him, the more he wanted, along with Michael.

I began to take Jason to the local YWCA to their therapeutic swim program. The center provided a time slot for families to bring their children who benefited the experience of aquatic therapy. I knew Jason loved the water, and I also knew the water would help relax his muscles.

One day while Jason and I were in the pool, Mrs. Ginny Thornburgh, the wife of our current Governor at that time, Dick Thornburgh, toured the center and stopped at the aquatic area to see the children. The photographer arranged for Mrs. Thornburgh to take a picture with one of the children. Of course they saw Jason laughing and having a good time. They called us over and asked if I would not mind if Jason took a picture with Mrs. Thornburgh.

"Of course not," I answered. "Jason loves to be in the spot light," I continued to say as I handed Jason to Mrs. Thornburgh. I was watching the interaction, was reading Jason's thoughts with his facial expressions, "Why am I being taken out of the water? I like the warm water. Oh, someone wants to take my picture, okay, but please put me back in the water so I can be held again by my mom and have some more fun." She handed him back to me and Jason continued to relax while I was slowly holding him with his back to my chest securing him under his arms as I swayed him slowly around the warm water.

Many times at home I would leave Jason on the floor on his belly and he would scoot using his arms to move his body around the room. One day, I was in the kitchen and I heard a moaning sound from the living room. I walked into the room and found Jason half-way under the couch. He wasn't crying and he did not appear to be scared; just trying to get my attention because he needed help to be moved from under the couch. He had more exploring to do.

He also lifted his head attempting to see what was on television. He liked anything with action and lots of color. We had a portable television, and it sat on a small table. Unfortunately, Jason was unable to pick his head up high enough to see the television.

On one occasion, while my parents were at our house, they were watching Jason attempting to look at the television. After their visit and when they returned to Florida, we received a check in the mail for $500.00 with a note asking us to buy a console TV so Jason could watch television. My parents were so special. I cannot express enough what their love and support meant to me.

It was Super Ball Sunday, and we invited my sister and her family over to enjoy the game and have a football style dinner with us. We were having so much fun. Allen decided Jason was going to be the kicker because his legs were shaped perfectly to kick the small football. Daddy held Jason using his leg to kick the ball, and the kids ran after the ball. The adults were laughing along with the kids, and Jason almost choked from laughing so hard. Later on that day, I was sitting on the couch watching the interactions of Michael and Jason with their cousins, Barry and Rena, and feeling so proud they accepted Jason in their lives so unconditionally.

Political Action

Jason appeared to love the United Cerebral Palsy Early Intervention Program. It was now two years since he started the program. It was similar to Ken Crest; difference being a full day program with more attention to physical and occupational therapy. In addition, he now had four more hours for range of motion therapy he desperately needed to help keep his muscles loose.

In a progress note received soon after Jason arrived at UCPA Early Intervention Program, it read, "Jason is adjusting well to the program, and he is a sociable child and loves attention. He will smile and babble to his classmates. Jason will respond with a smile when his name is called, and when a teacher asked him, 'Where is your mother and brother?' he would become so excited, moving his arms and legs sporadically. This is his way of responding to excitement." The report continued to say, "He tolerates his afternoon nap and will moan when he is disturbed from his nap. It is clear Jason loves to sleep."

He began to eat chopped food and was beginning to drink liquids with a thickening agent that helped to control his swallowing without choking. Eventually, he advanced to drinking liquids without the added thickening agent. His swallowing was improving but extra precautions were taken to be sure he didn't aspirate, he still was considered to be a high risk for aspiration.

Jason started showing love for music. We played music at home, and he would smile and appeared to enjoy listening to the different beats and the sounds of the music. The children received music therapy in school. I was told it was Jason's favorite time of the day. He would choose the instrument he wanted to play and would follow the other children with their instruments listening to the music. Of course, Jason needed hand over hand help with the activity.

It was a family myth we shared through the years in regards to music and singing. My dear mother-in-law had a beautiful singing voice and would sing while she was puttering in the kitchen. It was very obvious to all of us neither of her sons or our son Michael had a decent singing voice. However, because Jason loved music so much, we decided Jason was hiding a secret. He had a beautiful voice just like his Bubby. We would often joke with him about this, and he would smile like he knew the secret.

As you can see, Jason was a very lovable child. Everyone who had any contact with him loved him immediately. However, when he would be approached by someone he didn't know who looked threatening to him for some reason, he would stare at them to see if they presented any harm to him. He definitely was aware of his surroundings and familiar with people he had daily contact with. He was diagnosed as severely mentally retarded. Allen and I did not agree with this diagnosis, and we clearly made our feelings known. The standard for diagnosing severe mental retardation was based on severe physical disability involving the entire body including the inability to communicate. We understood, because of the above assessment, Jason was unable to learn and therefore the diagnosis of severe mental retardation was an appropriate assessment for Jason. We were told if Jason was not diagnosed with severe mental retardation, he would not be eligible to receive funding for early intervention and additional funding he may need access to in the future. We understood the premise and, therefore, accepted it. Apparently, it was all about bureaucratic policies and standards to assure the best care for Jason. We were very grateful for the opportunity for Jason to get the needed care we could not afford to pay.

With Jason attending UCPA, like Ken Crest, I was now involved with the Parent's Association. I was elected president of the association, and I organized a political action committee.

There were many problems related to potential spending cuts for early intervention programs. The committee was organized to work together as a group to contact our congressmen and senators to write letters requesting support for Title I PL 89-313 related to physical, speech, and occupational therapy for our children in early intervention programs along with parent educational programs. I wrote three letters to my politicians representing the state of Pennsylvania—Congressman Dougherty, Senator Spector, and Senator Heinz. I also wrote a letter directly to President Regan.

Because I was the president of the parents' support group and organized the political action committee, I attended two hearings. One hearing was scheduled on March 24, 1983, organized by Max Pievsky, who was my democratic member of the Pennsylvania House of Representatives. This was a public hearing for the allocation of funds for early intervention programs. Jason was with me and was sitting by my side while I pleaded to the members of the committee. I asked them not to cut access for therapy our children desperately needed. I pleaded our children needed therapy as early as possible in order to help them get a head start in life and give them a chance to succeed. I ended my speech saying, "Jason is with me today to give me the courage to tell you his story. As Jason's mother, I feel it is my responsibility to show the public that these children do exist and that they deserve to live a healthy and prosperous life. Jason doesn't want your pity; he just wants the chance to live a normal life."

The speech ended with an astounding applause that totally took me by surprise. I was so involved in the moment, I was not aware of the crowd around me.

I was getting ready to leave and was wheeling Jason toward the door when I was approached by a reporter from the local Channel News Station in Philadelphia. She stopped me to say, "I would like to follow you home so that I can interview you and Jason."

I looked at her somewhat surprised. I responded, "Oh, you do? Okay, sure. Here is my address, and I will meet you at my house.

"Oh my god," was my first reaction. "Jason, we are going to be on TV!"

After securing Jason in the car and driving home, a thought occurred to me. *Is my house clean?* I realized the reality, Jason and I were going to be on television and only then did I start feeling nervous. However, how could I possibly refuse the attention television access could give our cause.

Jason and I were on the local news that evening. We were now local celebrities.

A few days later, I found an article in the *Philadelphia Inquirer* written by a reporter who attended the hearing. He quoted a portion of my speech. He wrote, "When I brought Jason home from the hospital, I was scared. I didn't know how I would love this child. She enrolled the boy in an early intervention program where she learned to accept his handicap and also help him to develop his fullest potential. Jason doesn't want your pity today. He just wants a chance to live a normal life, she said to a thundering applause from the audience." Along with the television interview and the article in the Philadelphia newspaper, everyone began calling and congratulating us.

On November 21, 1983, I was asked to attend another hearing. Now I am representing our parents from the United Cerebral Palsy Support Group. The purpose for this speech was to express our feelings about why early intervention should be mandated throughout the state so that all Pennsylvania's handicapped children would benefit by the program.

I strongly verbalized in this speech, "Wouldn't it be beneficial for the State of Pennsylvania to mandate early intervention to encourage families in our state to provide a warm and loving family environment for their handicapped child versus institutionalization?"

Jason was going to leave United Cerebral Palsy and begin public school. Before Jason's graduation, he was evaluated for placement in a classroom in the Philadelphia School District. In 1975, the Congress passed a law providing an education for all children. This law, "Individuals with Disabilities Education Act" (IDEA) strongly impacted many disabled individuals.

Jason was evaluated, and he was placed in a severely and profoundly impaired (SPI) classroom at a public school near our home. Nancy's daughter Abby was placed in the same classroom.

Since 1986, the language used to classify our children was changed many times through the years. Many parents complained about the discriminatory language used in classifications. In my opinion, severely and profoundly impaired, in today's standards, would be considered discriminatory and would never have been accepted.

Michael

In September 1985 a new phase in the life of my boys began, attending the Philadelphia Public School System. I was thankful to whoever scheduled the school buses for the special education children. Jason was scheduled to be picked up first. Thankfully, this allowed me time to take Michael to school without any delay. Michael was enrolled in the half day morning kindergarten at our local school that was in walking distance from our house.

Michael looked so cute with his new school clothes and a backpack when I dropped him off for his first day at kindergarten.

I had the opportunity to meet his kindergarten teacher prior to the beginning of school, and I told her about his medical history and that he was receiving occupational therapy at Easter Seals. I did not tell her my concerns of probable learning problems based on what the nursery school teacher shared with me. She approached me at his graduation from nursery school and advised me to watch him carefully. It was her opinion that he was behind his peers in several levels.

I decided not to tell her this because I felt if he was behind his peers in several levels, I wanted her to observe Michael with an open mind and not to look for something that may not be there. She thanked me and said she would keep an eye on Michael and give me periodic updates as to how he is doing in kindergarten.

Six months into the school term, Michael's kindergarten teacher contacted me. She strongly suggested I request an evaluation for special education before he starts first grade. She told me, "He is a very quiet and pleasant child and tends to be a loner. After six months getting acquainted with him, I find him to be falling behind his peers in his classroom. He will often play quietly and shy away from difficult tasks. He is slowly falling behind in classroom activities, not wanting to attempt a task if it is difficult."

I called the school counselor. Apparently, Michael's teacher also reported her findings to the counselor as well.

I was sitting in her office, and she abruptly spurts out, "It is not our policy to evaluate children at a kindergarten level!" She continues, "You have to wait until Michael starts first grade."

I was clearly upset and responded abruptly back to her, "Michael was evaluated by an occupational therapist and is receiving occupational therapy at Easter Seals!"

I showed her the reports I brought documenting his medical history. I also had an occupational therapy report and referring letter from his therapist at Easter Seals.

I told her, "All of my documentation should serve as justification to evaluate him now. In addition, I do not want him to be subjected to potential problems and delays when he starts first grade in September. I also do not want to subject Michael to any discomfort from his peers if he is not keeping up as noted by his kindergarten teacher!"

However, it is like talking to a brick wall. She refused to budge and stood behind her bureaucratic hypocrisy, and she simply "pissed me off" big time. If this was an example of red tape, I would be buried under because of strong-minded bureaucrats who make decisions. I had a lot to learn.

Unfortunately, I did not continue the fight and I allowed Michael to finish kindergarten without an evaluation. I had a feeling there would be many more battles for both boys, and

I could not fight each one; I needed to pick my battles worth fighting. I did not have the strength to deal with it all.

When the school bus arrived to pick Jason up for school for the first day, he looked so cute in his new school clothes sitting in his wheelchair with his school bag attached. The bus driver opened the school bus door and operated the lift to bring it down to street level, and I wheeled Jason onto the lift. I watched Jason's expression of wonder. He quickly started to giggle with enjoyment as the lift raised him to the bus entrance. It appeared he liked the new ride. I can tell he wanted more as I watched his expression while his wheelchair was being secured. After Jason was secured on the bus, the driver turned to me and told me he was surprised to see such a happy child on the first day of school. *Oh yes,* I thought. This bus driver just met a new friend; a special child with an outgoing personality. Jason also met a new friend who has the ability to take him on a special ride.

I also had the opportunity to meet Jason's teacher before the beginning of the semester. I met Mr. Frankelwich, who was assigned to be Jason's teacher. We met at a meeting to plan Jason's Individual Educational Plan (IEP).

All special education students were required to establish an IEP. An IEP was a contract between the school personnel and the special needs child and his family. Jason's IEP required him to be in a classroom with one teacher and two aides. After meeting Mr. Frankelwich, I immediately knew he and Jason would get along just fine.

Jason's daily schedule consisted of activities based on his IEP goals and daily range of motion. He had a planned daily schedule for a week laid out that included music, art, auditorium time with the entire school and gym. Jason's classroom was in a regular elementary school and children from the neighborhood attended the school. Jason's special education class was the only one in this school. Occasionally, a group of the non-special education students were invited to assist in Jason's classroom and I welcomed the interaction with the "normal" students. I believed the children needed to be exposed at an early age and to understand there are special needs children in their school and not to be scared of them. This policy proved to be a very positive experience for the children, educators, and the special needs child.

During the summer months, both boys attended summer camp. Jason went to the Easter Seals camp and thankfully was transported by bus. I was very thankful Easter Seals provided a camp for special needs children. As an alternative, Jason was eligible to attend public school in the summer. The public school summer program was a half-day session three times per week, and it did not extend through the full summer. I wanted the best care for Jason to assure he would not regress during the summer. I also liked the idea he would be outside and have the opportunity to swim.

During the next school semester, Jason returned to his classroom, and Michael began first grade at the local elementary school. I was anxious to see how Michael would react to first grade both emotionally and educationally since my request to have him evaluated the previous school year was denied.

One month after school started, I received a phone call from Michael's first grade teacher. She told me Michael will be transferred to a transitional classroom because it was her opinion he was not keeping up with the rest of the children educationally. She contacted the same counselor I had issues with the previous year, and together, they both recommended he be evaluated for special education. Of course I was angry and I clearly let them know how I felt. I respected Michael's teacher for her quick assessment of his apparent problems. Just let me clarify my feelings in just one sentence—Never underestimate the power of a mother who cares for a special needs child." This statement says it all, and nothing more needs to be said other than I learned a powerful lesson.

Michael's new classroom was referred to as a transitional room. It was a classroom where they placed children who were having trouble keeping up with their peers in a regular classroom and were waiting for an evaluation and/or a new placement in a special education setting. It was a small class, and Michael loved the one-on-one attention he was receiving. He got along well with both the teacher and the aide assigned to the class. The aide in the class was a wonderful person who worked with Michael closely. Michael was a delightful child and was easily loved by anyone who took their time to get to know him. He was an introverted child and one-on-one teaching worked for him, and he was starting to blossom in the classroom.

The evaluation was completed and Michael's tests results found him to be mildly learning disabled. The IEP meeting was scheduled, and we agreed with the IEP contract that included occupational therapy.

Michael continued special education throughout elementary, middle, and high school.

When Michael started high school, he had the opportunity to attend a technical school, and he decided to check out the curriculum. He really liked what they offered him. He decided to take food services. His day was split with book learning in the morning at his high school and technical school classes in the afternoon. Michael's decision to attend the technical school to take food service proved to be a life changing decision for him. His food service teacher, Mr. Levin, was a great teacher. He became his mentor and a true friend who was very supportive. I am so grateful to Mr. Levin. He truly brought Michael out of his shell and helped him become the wonderful man he is today. He helped him gain confidence he desperately needed and only a great teacher could do this. Michael loved food services, and he made many friends he could relate to. Michael applied to both the Culinary Institute of America outside of New York and the Johnson and Wales University in Providence, Rhode Island. He was accepted to both schools and chose to go to the Culinary Institute of America.

I continued to try hard to make our family life as normal as possible. We were involved in many activities throughout the year including attending Michael's little league baseball games. As a family, special events such as "Hands across America" and United Cerebral Palsy Telethons became part of our life's activities.

Handling and caring for Jason was starting to drain Allen and me both physically and emotionally. He was getting older and bigger.

During the day, when I was alone, I had to pull Jason's wheelchair up two flights of stairs in front of our house because the school bus driver was not allowed to help due to insurance issues. My hands were beginning to develop welts from lifting the wheelchair. Occasionally, if one of my neighbors was available, they would assist me; otherwise, I had to do it myself.

During Jason's second semester in public school, the bus schedule was changed. He now was the last child to be dropped off at home. Michael's school day ended the same time Jason was due to arrive home. Since I could not be at two places at one time, it created a problem for me.

I contacted the school district to request a different drop off time for Jason, but they refused to change it. I could not have asked any of my neighbors to take Jason up the two flights of stairs in his wheelchair for me.

Fortunately, I became friends with the school crossing guard at Michael's school. She offered for Michael to stay with her and help her cross the children until I was able to drive over with Jason to pick him up. I graciously accepted her offer.

This was when I realized the differences in our family and the unusual circumstances we had to live with. When Jason arrived home, I immediately placed him in our minivan. We adapted our minivan by removing the middle seat so we could place the wheelchair and securely attach it to the van. Jason's wheelchair had one large wheel in the front and two wheels in the back. I tilted the chair back so the front wheel reached the van, and then I pushed the wheelchair in the van. I quickly drove over to pick up Michael. When we all arrived home, I removed Jason from the van and pulled him up two flights of stairs into the house.

Having to perform this routine every school day was not easy, and my arms, hands, legs, and back were starting to feel the strain. Carrying Jason upstairs and giving him a bath was also difficult. Of course, at night, Allen was a great help and took some of the burden off of me. However, it was getting difficult for him as well, especially after working a full day. I suppose you can say I worked all day too, and I was tired as well. We both had good reasons to be tired, and we did not see any way out of our situation.

Jason was due for his six-month evaluation with Dr. Brown. The appointment with Dr. Brown turned out to be a life-changing, agonizing visit I will never forget it. It made an impact in our family's future and Jason's welfare.

Family Challenges

It was 1985, and the day to day caring for our dear son was becoming more and more difficult. He was getting heavier and increasingly harder to lift and carry up and down the stairs. I cared for him the majority of the time. The physical strain on my body was becoming apparent dragging his wheelchair up and down the outside steps. Changing his diapers and dressing him was difficult because of his spasticity (stiffness in all muscles). Positioning him was important. I needed to change his position periodically throughout the day to avoid sores on his body and to avoid joint contractures (tightness in his joints that could cause muscle and bone damage). He was moved from a sitting position in his wheelchair, to the floor on his back, his side or stomach. His head needed to be supported with every position I placed him in because it was his natural instinct to force his neck and head to the left with his arms up close to his body. It was important to try and maneuver him to avoid his natural position because it only increased his spasticity in his head, neck and chest. His entire body was affected by his spasticity. His legs were atrophied due to his immobility.

Dad joined me when I took Jason for his six month neurologic assessment with Dr. Brown. After he examined Jason, he asked to speak with me in his office.

After dressing Jason and placing him in his wheelchair, we all entered his office and found Dr. Brown carefully looking over Jason's chart. Knowing Dr. Brown as well as I did for the past six years, he never invited me to his office. While observing his body language and facial expression, it appeared he had something on his mind and was trying to find the right words to express his thoughts.

He looked directly at me and said, "It is now six years since I first met you and Jason. I am going over his chart and reading my notes, and it is apparent to me Jason's condition is not improving. In fact, he is showing more signs of severe impairment. I decided not to talk with you at our last appointment so I could continue to assess Jason's progress with the hope I would see improvement. However, there is no improvement in Jason's muscle tone. I now believe his body will deteriorate further as he continues to get older."

He took my hand when he saw my eyes tearing and looked directly into my eyes, "This will create a great amount of stress on you, Allen, and Michael. I believe you and Allen have proved to be wonderful parents and did everything you can to make Jason's life comfortable. However, it is time to consider placing Jason in an institution where he can get the medical care he needs."

With each word spoken from his mouth, my body responded. I became anxious, scared, and increasingly angry listening to each and every word. I was in shock. I looked at him, trying to stay calm. I eventually found my voice again and carefully chose my words and proceeded to say, "I will never place Jason in an institution. He is our son, and we want him home with us!" My dear father knew not to interfere and just sat beside me keeping his thoughts to himself.

I thanked him for his honesty and his professional opinion and picked myself up and walked out of the office with Jason.

Dad and I drove home in silence. I decided not to say anything to Allen because I needed time to absorb Dr. Brown's assessment of Jason.

His words became embedded in my mind, and I could not forget what he said. I spent the next few weeks trying to sort it all out. It cluttered my soul, my dreams; I could not forget it. I eventually reached the conclusion—Dr. Brown was right. He knew I would give up my whole life to care for Jason, and he was trying to help me. It occurred to me he knew I would react this way and I also realized if he placed the thought in my head, I would eventually sort it out and reach the conclusion, it was the only choice we had. He was right. We could not continue living the way we were. Our entire life was involved in the caring for Jason 24/7. We had no social life. Michael was a quiet introverted child who needed our attention. Our financial situation was a constant struggle.

I found a job as a medical transcriptionist working from home. The pay was minimal. Additionally, it was hard to concentrate or find the time to work without getting interrupted. I eventually found another job at a mental health facility working as an administrative assistant. The hours were flexible, and I was able to work while the boys were in school. It was a good job but the pay was not helping our financial situation. I needed to return to work full-time.

If we hired a nurse to care for Jason, it would take all of my salary to pay her wages. In addition, our house was not handicapped accessible, and we could not afford to move without my contribution working full time. Jason was under Allen's medical insurance. He was not eligible for Medicaid because Allen's salary was over the limit for their standards. Our health insurance did not pay for equipment Jason needed. It boiled down to one basic fact: we would not get the support needed as long as Jason was living at home. I was having a difficult time accepting this. Why couldn't someone see we needed help to care for our child in our home? Why was the only option to place Jason in an institution?

After diligently researching information, I found placing Jason in an institution would give him eligibility for full funding. This included room and board, all medical needs including equipment, 24/7 nursing care, and he would be eligible for Medicaid and SSI. This was the reality of our mental health/mental retardation system. Basically, it opened my eyes to the nonexistence of available support from our city, state, or federal government. The powers to be were willing to fund Jason in an institution. They would completely care for his needs in an institution rather than providing funding for Jason to live at home with his family. This just did not make sense. However, I finally caved in after much soul searching and faced the hard fact; there just was no alternative.

One night after the boys went to bed, I finally opened up to Allen about Dr. Brown's visit and what he told me. I explained what I found after researching. We thoroughly discussed the impact of Jason living at home with us compared to sending him to an institution. We went over the pros and cons of both scenarios and ultimately reached, what we both believed, to be the only solution—place Jason in an institution.

I did not begin my search until I discussed our decision with my parents. I was afraid of admitting to anyone we wanted to place Jason in an institution, especially my parents. Allen planned on talking to his parents alone as I chose to with my parents. Allen's mom and dad did not outwardly interfere with any of our decisions. I was aware Allen's mom was opinioned, but I also knew she would not attempt to change our minds because it was such a personal decision. I did know she would not make the choice to institutionalize her son if it was up to her.

A few days later, after building up the courage, I visited my parents. I walked into the house, sat down, and promptly blurted out, "What would you think of me if I placed Jason in an institution?"

My father and mother looked at each other and my father said, "It is about time you made this decision." We hugged each other, and I walked out of their house feeling so much better.

If all of the above was not enough to make my life unbearable, my father called me at work about a month later and asked if I would stop at their house on my way home. I entered their house, and my father was in the living room alone.

He asked me to sit down and told me, "Mom has leukemia. It is a very rare form, and she will have to start treatment immediately."

With my life solely occupied with Jason's needs and dealing with him leaving, my ability to feel emotion was just not happening. I felt like a zombie most of the time living in a world of nonexistence. I took each blow as it came not unlike a punching bag, picking myself up and continuing on. It was my defense mechanism protecting myself from feeling anything. This terrible news was another punch to my inner soul challenging my strength and ability to survive.

I found my mom in the kitchen. I walked in, and she hugged me hard and cried, "I do not want to die."

I don't want her to die either, I thought as I held her tight. I did not cry! *There it is again*, I thought, *the damn defense mechanism, no feelings*. I did not console her, other than hugging her. This is what I could do but I could not cry with her. I wanted to and should have but I did not feel emotion.

Mom started her treatment a few weeks later, and Dad became her full-time caregiver. He was a wonderful husband and was devoted to her completely.

I started researching institutions for Jason. I called the Philadelphia Office of Mental Health and Mental Retardation. The woman on the phone told me there weren't any funds available in Philadelphia County. She referred me to the State Office of Mental Health and Mental Retardation.

I called the state office, and she laid out options available for Jason. She said, "There are several institutions throughout the state of Pennsylvania. They are referred to as Intermediate Care Facilities (ICF/IID), which is defined as, 'ICF/IID funding for individuals with intellectual disabilities or other related conditions such as severe and profoundly impaired children/adults.' I have a list of these facilities, and I will mail a copy to you."

Allen and I narrowed the list to a few located close to our home. We started visiting the homes. I detested referring to these facilities as "institutions" and would prefer to call them either "centers" or "homes." We found a home located in Abbottstown, Pennsylvania, ten miles south of Gettysburg, which was a two-and-a-half hour one-way trip from Philadelphia. The name of the home was Children's Developmental Center. All four of us drove the five hour round trip to visit the home.

We were impressed immediately as we entered the building. It was clean and odorless. I called and spoke with Pennie Spalding a week or so earlier to schedule a time and day, and she met us at the entrance. Pennie Spalding was the administrator. We talked with Pennie for a long time. She clarified the services available for the residents living there. She offered us a tour, and as we walked through the building, I noticed the residents to be of varying ages. A few appeared to be around Jason's age. The personal aides we met during the tour appeared to be kind and devoted to their clients. The building sat on a large lot surrounded by farm land. The air was clear of smog which provided a wonderful country atmosphere. We liked the idea of Jason living in the country away from the hustle and bustle of the city.

After our visit to the Children's Developmental Center, Allen and I listed the pros and cons related to Jason possibly living there. With much thought and deep soul searching we agreed this was the best place for Jason.

I called the State Office of Mental Health and Mental Retardation. She told me there was a waiting list, and Jason would be placed on the list. When I asked this woman how long the list was, she would not tell me or even give me an estimate of how long it would take for a bed to be available. After finally making the most difficult decision in our lives and placing Jason on the waiting list, there was nothing else to do but wait.

Mom, on the other hand, completed her treatments and at her last doctors' visit; she was told the leukemia was in remission. We all were so relieved and thankful. It was a terrible disease, and it took a toll on Mom.

It was November of 1985. Mom and Dad were ready to return to the warmth of Florida. With Mom in remission and getting away from the cold winter, we were in a better frame of mind. We said our good-byes and prayed mom would gain back her strength after her long ordeal with the cancer treatments.

Facing Death

My parents returned to Florida, and both boys started their second school term. While the boys were in school, I continued to work part-time at a job I enjoyed. It provided the opportunity to get out of the house, communicate with adults, and of course, help with our finances. We talked to Mom and Dad regularly, and Mom regained her strength and vitality enjoying the warmth of Florida and her social life playing mahjong and attending her favorite past time, the Saturday night dances she enjoyed so much. I was happy and relieved she was doing so well.

Allen lost his job, and I had to take Jason to the Medicaid office to apply for medical assistance to cover his medical expenses since we no longer had health insurance. This just added to the many burdens and the daily tension I was living with. With my job and the unemployment checks Allen received, it was still not enough to live with, and it was adding to our already overwhelming tension. Of course, both our parents were helping as much as they could. We were so fortunate to have the support of our family, and I did not know what we would have done without them.

Allen and I were certainly feeling the pressure, and it was taking a toll on our marriage. We were beginning to lose patience with each other. With me acting as mother, advocate, nurse, and therapist, it was certainly inundating. Most importantly, I had another son who needed my attention as well. He was such a good boy and never complained. This scared me. He didn't open up to ask me why I could not take him to school, why I always had to take care of Jason, why can't I take him to the playground without taking Jason along? It was undoubtedly unfair for him to not have a "normal" family life, especially not having a twin brother he could relate to. Life wasn't fair!

It was unfortunate Allen lost his job, but in some ways, it was helpful. He was now home to help me care for Jason during the weekdays. He was extremely helpful just by getting Jason up in the morning, dressing him, and bringing him downstairs. He fed him breakfast and brought him down the stairs to the awaiting school bus.

It was a blessing, however, when Allen was offered a job. Of course I was grateful and happy for him to be employed again. However, I lost my wonderful support I so appreciated while he was home. The new position included full benefits along with health insurance. We were so grateful they did not consider Jason's condition preexisting.

I am aware I may have sounded selfish at times when I referred to the effects and burden of the daily care we provided for Jason. Please understand it came with the territory. I loved my son with all my heart and soul, but I needed to be honest with myself as well. I was tired, scared, and frustrated. When I got out of bed to face another day, the burden continued. Allen and I did not have a normal married life with two normal children. This was what we faced daily. I used the strength God gave me to make it through each day.

On a positive side, caring for my sweet child was rewarding in so many ways, especially with Jason's pleasant disposition. We played with both boys equally like most parents did with their children. Jason was not intimidated with any type of rough playing. He actually waited patiently for his turn and when I approached, he kicked and threw his arms about anticipating the fun.

The Jewish holiday, Hanukkah, was a big deal in our immediate and extended family. Allen's mom always host the party since I traditionally cooked Thanksgiving dinner for everyone. Hanukkah was a wonderful and happy celebration with lighting the candles, playing with the dreidel (a traditional game played with a spinning toy with four sides), and of course, opening the gifts. Gift opening was the best part of the party. All the kids sat on the floor, and eventually, the floor was covered with wrapping papers, ribbons, and bows.

This year, we actually lost Jason amongst the array of unwrapped gifts. We heard him giggling with joy and found him under a large piece of wrapping paper. During the day, while watching television, both Barry and Rena (my nephew and niece) sat on the floor with the boys. Barry supported Jason against his chest so Jason could watch television as well.

Allen and I considered ourselves extremely lucky. Every member, both sides of our family, accepted and loved Jason unconditionally. I heard stories from members of my support group. They told me stories about their families who did not want anything to do with their disabled family member, as if they were going to catch the "disease!" Our friends and neighbors accepted Jason as a loving and charming young boy.

It was difficult to socialize with our friends because of the obvious challenges taking Jason with us. However, we did have an occasion when we all climbed into the van and drove to south Jersey where we met our very good friends, Judith and Gerald and their family at a restaurant. While we were enjoying our dinner and catching up with each other's lives, Jason sat quietly listening and observing. When we left the restaurant saying our good-byes, Allen removed Jason from his wheelchair to place him in the car seat. How surprised we were when we found a few pieces of silverware tucked into the side of his chair.

I looked directly into Jason's eyes and asked him, "How did you hide the silverware in your chair without anyone seeing you?"

He responded to me with one of his typical facial expression emanating guilt, and it appeared it could be translated to "I did it!" He followed this look with a big smile. He never ceased to amaze me.

Allen returned the silverware to the manager and apologized for Jason's behavior. She laughed with amazement and was very gracious and accepted the silverware except for one spoon, which she handed over to Allen. She told Allen, "I have a cousin who is disabled like your son. However, he does not have the ability to do what your son just did. I would like him to keep this spoon as a gift from me." From this day forward, Jason was now known as the kleptomaniac in the Quate family.

Allen's father was an excellent wood crafter, and he built Jason a large table that was at the level of Allen and my heights. This helped us to change Jason without straining our backs.

He also built us, what was referred to as a "side-lier" in the physical therapy world. It was a very simple but valuable therapy tool consisting of two flat pieces of wood attached in an L shape. Jason would be placed on his side, at the intersection where the wood pieces met. He was secured in place with a leather belt. Because he was lying in this position his arms are faced forward in front of him aligned where his hands touched. We would place a pillow behind his head so his eyes were aligned to see his hands working together attempting to reach for an object hanging or lying in front of him. Therapeutically it served as a good source to practice cognitive skills and eye and hand coordination. If he touched something and he caused it to move or make a sound, this would help him understand cause and effect. Jason's positioning had to be changed every couple of hours to assure good range of motion, and help keep his muscles loose to avoid sores on his body.

When I returned home from work and before Jason and Michael would arrive home from school, I would often sit and meditate. There was absolutely no time for me to cry and feel sorry for myself and what good would this do me anyway. I could not cry anyway as I mentioned earlier.

It is so hard to explain what I was feeling. Let me try by using the analogy of splitting myself into two people sitting on each of my shoulders. They are arguing against each other. The Judy on the right shoulder argued, "Let Jason go so he can receive the proper nursing care he needs and you can start living a normal family life."

However, the other Judy would argue back, "I am his mother and should dedicate the rest of my life to his care. I love him; he needs to be with his family."

I was crying silent tears just thinking about how my need for him to leave our home was overriding the need to keep him home safe with us. I saw myself to be a very selfish mother, and I hated myself.

I literally could not keep up with the never-ending monthly bills. I did not want to lose our house, and I was scared to death of what the future held for our family. I was so stressed out with all of these thoughts in my head, and I would sit meditating and praying to God for strength and guidance.

The only alternative I had was to begin writing letters to everyone I could think of. This included our congressman and senator. I also wrote an emotional letter to Pennie Spalding, the woman who we met at Children's Developmental Center. I begged her to please help us. I spilled out all of my fears hoping she would find a way to help me. The only letter I received in response was from Congressman Borski's office who was our democratic congressman in the district where we lived. I saw some light at the end of the tunnel after I talked to one of his associates. She was very compassionate and promised to see what their office could do to help.

It was the beginning of spring, and Mom and Dad were on their way home from Florida. They were my support system, and I needed them very badly since I felt I was beginning to fall apart.

The day they arrived home, I walked into their house eagerly to see them. I entered the front door, and they were both sitting in the living room. I looked at my mom and saw something in her eyes I didn't like. She told me the worse possible news. Her doctor in Florida urged her to immediately see her Philadelphia Oncologist upon returning home to Philadelphia. It appeared her remission has ended and the leukemia returned. I suppose somewhere in the back of my mind I knew the remission was not permanent, but I refused to think about it.

Mom immediately started her treatments again. After several sessions with blood transfusions and drugs, her blood levels did not change. A new medicine recently approved in the USA was offered to Mom and she agreed to take it. This new medicine was extremely expensive, very lethal, and she was warned it can produce severe side-effects. Mom started getting very sick immediately after just a few days on the medicine.

In the meantime, I heard from the county office in Philadelphia. They offered assistance to relieve the strain we were under. The assistance consisted of equipment we did not need and the availability of respite care. Respite care was a program available for families who have children who are physically disabled. It gives them an opportunity to leave their child so the family could have a few days of respite. We did use this service a few times, and Jason appeared to receive good care.

The woman from Congressman Borski's office called occasionally to inform me Jason's name was moving up the long waiting list. This occurred every time inquiries were initiated regarding Jason's welfare either to the State Office of Mental Health/Mental Retardation or the Children's Developmental Center. Apparently, Congressman Borski's office was making a difference.

Early in October, Mom became very weak and mostly slept through the day. I needed someone to watch Jason for me because I had to take Michael somewhere. Dad offered to watch Jason. I argued with him because I felt he had enough on his plate already and he did not need the extra burden of watching Jason as well. However, Dad told me it was mom's request. She wanted to see Jason; I agreed reluctantly.

When I returned to their house, I found Jason sleeping on one side of their sofa and Mom sleeping on the other side with dad sitting on the chair watching both of them. I left there with a sinking feeling, somewhat strange; almost as if mom needed to see Jason one last time.

Just a few weeks later, Mom was admitted to the hospital in a weakened condition. She developed an ulcer on her lower right leg that wasn't healing because of her compromised immune system from the leukemia. The medicine was not helping. In fact, it put her in a weakened condition, in my opinion. I was watching my mother suffering, and it was breaking my heart. Their doctor highly recommended amputating her right leg. I struggled with the decision. I felt deep in my soul my mom was dying, and I did not feel amputation was necessary.

My mom was a very proud and dignified woman. If she had the fight still in her to say no, I believe she would have. However, the doctor performed the surgery. Mom apparently was giving up. I wanted her to die in peace with her whole body intact.

Just a few days before Thanksgiving, Mom was transferred to the Intensive Care Unit. The three of us, Arlene, Dad, and I waited in the ICU waiting room all night. Mom was only allowed one visitor at a time so we chose to stay all night and take turns sitting by her side holding her hand.

When it was my turn to see Mom, I found her thrashing around in her bed with her body exposed. I covered her and turned to the nurse. "Why is she thrashing so much? My mother is a proud woman and would not want her body to be exposed," I told her.

"Your mom is fighting a battle to live and thrashing around in her bed is her way of fighting the battle. She is in pain. We are giving her medicine but it is not enough," she responded.

"Can we can give her something stronger? I do not want my mom to be in so much pain, she suffered enough in the last three months."

Apparently, the nurse contacted mom's doctor, and they increased the pain medicine that placed mom in a coma. On November 22, 1986, my dear, loving mom passed away. She no longer was suffering and was now in peace.

While planning her funeral and talking to the rabbi about mom's life, I remembered the day I left Jason with my parents. I now realized she was saying good-bye to her precious grandson whom she will never see again. She loved all of her grandchildren equally, but for obvious reasons, Jason was special.

God's Mysterious Ways

My beloved mom was buried the day after Thanksgiving. Immediately, after the service, we all gathered at my parent's home where we had a catered lunch served.

Traditionally, in our religion, the immediate family returns to the "Shiva" house where friends and family gather after the service to be served food and extend additional support. The "Shiva" house can be open to visitors from three days up to a week, depending on the grieving family's request.

We sat for three days and greeted many of mom's friends and our extended family members. I found myself sitting each day politely greeting our visitors. They arrived throughout each day periodically. My thoughts were wandering thinking about how I lost my best friend and my mentor. She was a wonderful wife, mother, and grandmother. I think about the sweet, loving woman my mother was for so many years, but as I greeted all of her friends through the last few days, I realized she had a fulfilling life. It suddenly hit me like a ton of bricks she is no longer with me. I will truly miss her.

A few weeks later, just before the holidays—Hanukah and New Year—Dad decided it was time to return to Florida and resume his life. The many years they were "snow birds" traveling back to Florida, they always drove. Because Dad would be driving alone this time, Allen and I both decided we were going with him.

All three of us (Michael, Allen and I) packed our bags into our car and followed Dad on the way to Florida. We left Jason in respite care we used in the past. We would be away from Jason for ten days, over the Christmas and New Year holidays. This was the longest time period we left Jason in their care. I felt uneasy leaving Jason for so long, but we made the decision to go and had no choice.

After arriving in Florida and helping Dad clean the apartment and shop for food, we settled and took the time to unwind and grieve. Dad did not express his feelings. After a few days, I became aware he was happy we drove with him just by his actions. He was actually smiling at times. Michael always made Pop-Pop smile. I felt an aura around him. He was not his usual pleasant self, however. He was dealing with losing his wife of forty-eight years. This had to be very difficult for him.

I called the respite facility to check up on Jason. I was told he was doing great. I asked to speak to him. All they had to do was place the phone by his ear so he could hear my voice. I knew this would be a comfort to him. I heard a strange voice on the phone who said, "Hi, Mom." Immediately, I responded with anger as I waited for the woman to return to the phone.

"This is not my son; he cannot talk," I told her. I was angry and confused. I continued to ask the woman on the phone, "Where is my son? Do you know who he is? Do you know he cannot talk?"

"Oh, I am so sorry," she responded. "Would you like me to find him for you?"

"Never mind," I said. "We will be leaving in a few days, and I will see him soon." I slammed the phone down on its receiver in anger. What can I do? I was too far away. After the phone call, I became anxious and couldn't wait to go home and see Jason.

One week after the dreadful phone call, we arrived home. We cleared the luggage from the car and immediately reentered the car to pick Jason up. We arrived at the apartment finding Jason lying on the sofa. I went over to him, picked him up in my arms, and he didn't respond to me.

"What is wrong with him?" I asked the woman on duty that day.

"What is your concern, Mrs. Quate? He is just fine," she responded. "He has been laying here on the sofa waiting for you to arrive to take him home."

"He is obviously not fine; he appears to be unconscious," I noted emphatically. I quickly walked out of the room with him cuddled in my arms.

We were driving to Allen's parents' home, and I was unable to elicit any response from him. His normal response after seeing us would be a lower lip pout that would extend down to his neck as if to say, "I am angry at you."

My anxiety was now in full motion. I started to undress him to examine his body. He was pale and it appeared he lost weight. When I found, what appeared to be cigarette burns on his knuckles, I was appalled. I looked at Jason and asked, "What happened to you, dear?"

We arrived at Allen's parent's home. My instincts told me to go there first because I felt I needed a second opinion before I took further steps. I was not thinking clearly because I should have asked Allen to take us directly to the emergency room. However, this was what we did.

Immediately after walking into the house, Mom approached me and took Jason from my arms. She looked at his closed eyes and immediately asked Allen to call the doctor. Within minutes, Allen had the doctor on the phone; he described Jason's condition to him. This gentle man of a doctor never hesitated to see Jason when any one of us would call him out of concern for Jason's welfare. He asked us to bring Jason to his house immediately, and Allen and I left for his house within two minutes.

While we were driving over to the doctor's house, Jason opened his eyes for a short time and looked at me like he was trying to tell me something.

"What happened to you?" I asked him.

I was imagining the worse scenarios. Was he abused? Was he deprived of food? He just stared at me with his eyes full of fear and closed them again.

We arrive at the doctor's home, and he took Jason from my arms and we followed him to his kitchen where he laid Jason down on his table. He took his vitals, checked his heart, and pinched his skin. He turned and reached for the phone and dialed. While waiting for the phone to answer on the other end, he picked up his hand and saw the burn marks on his knuckles and looked at me in disgust. "Hello, this is Dr. Steiker. I have a child at my house now that needs immediate attention. I am sending him directly to your emergency room for treatment. His parents will be bringing him there in a few minutes." He made his point and quickly returned the phone to its receiver.

Dr. Steiker turned to Allen and I while we were dressing Jason. "He appears to be severely dehydrated and is in a semi-conscious state. His condition is unstable. You take him directly to the emergency room, and I will meet you there later," he told us as we walked out the door.

We arrived at the emergency room, and the doctor quickly took Jason from my arms and ran him into the room and closed the door. Allen and I were anxiously waiting outside the room in an extremely agitated state, not believing what was happening.

Oh my god, I thought! *What did they do to my son?* I just sat with Allen, both of us in shock, in the cold, somewhat dreary hallway of the emergency room outside the room where they took Jason behind a closed door.

After an hour waiting outside the room, the doctor finally opened the door and approached us. "We will be transferring Jason to the intensive care unit in a few minutes," he said. "Your son's sodium count is extremely high. He is in a semi-conscious state because of the severity of his dehydration and extremely high sodium count. He needs to be watched closely in the intensive care unit.

"In comparison, let me describe his condition. Let's take a can of soup for example. This can of soup is very high in sodium. It would appear like someone forced fed him many cans of this soup for the entire ten days he was in their care. This would account for his very high sodium count. I am not saying this is what happened. I am only using the scenario as a comparison in order for you to understand the extreme state of his condition. We need to watch him very closely. If his sodium count drops too quickly, he will be in danger of possible liver or kidney failure. Do you know how he got these cigarette burns on his knuckles?"

"He was at a respite facility, and when we picked him up today, this is how we found him," I responded.

"I want you to know I believe Jason is a victim of abuse, and I am going to report this abuse to the authorities."

Allen and I drove home in silence. We arrived at my in-laws house and sat down to tell them what we now know. We were all in shock. My father-in-law was a quiet soul, but when he got angry, everyone outside of his home could hear him. He wanted to know.

"What the hell did they do to Jason!" he shouted.

My mother-in-law was shaking with fright. They loved Jason with all of their heart and soul, and you could feel their anger and fright in the atmosphere of the room.

After a few days in ICU, Jason's sodium count slowly lowered without any problems and finally showed normal levels. He was transferred out of ICU and finally discharged a week after he was admitted to the hospital.

We were so relieved to have Jason back in the comfort of our home and his beautiful smile and great disposition returned. His beautiful eyes reverted back with sparkles and the awareness he was known for. I will never forget the look he gave me when I asked him what happened to him. If only he could have told me, however, I will never know.

You better believe I am now one angry mother. I called the office of Mental Health and Mental Retardation in Philadelphia who offered the respite service to us. I told them, in so many words, what they could do with their respite care. I told the woman on the phone, "I will never take my son there again." I continued my rage, saying, "I will make sure I let everyone know not to take their children there either."

I also called our state senator and Congressman Borski's offices and gave them the same earful. There was no stopping me. I was simply a "pissed off mother," and I will let everyone know how I felt. I was sure some of this rage was due to mourning my mom, but it did not take away the fact what happened to Jason.

A few weeks later, we received a certified letter in the mail stating, "After thoroughly investigating the charges of abuse that was reported by the emergency room doctor, our findings prove to be unfounded."

It was my interpretation their findings were based on a child who was severely and profoundly impaired. Most likely they concluded and based their findings on Jason developing an illness while in the care of the respite facility. The report did not mention the cigarette burns on his knuckles. How could this be? My child was taken directly from the care at a respite center to an ICU in a hospital with burn marks on his knuckles, and they reported it to be unfounded. Something was wrong here. I saw a "cover-up." I also saw a disability discrimination incident. However, I did not have the strength or the ability to fight a lost cause so we just left it alone and continued to live our lives like nothing happened.

A few weeks later, I received a phone call from Pennie Spalding informing me there was a bed available for Jason. I believe Congressman Borski and his staff pressured the Children's Developmental Center to place Jason on top of the list. I believed everyone involved was now aware of Jason's "incident" and through an " act of God," someone had to own up to a tragic incident and provide the bed for Jason. This was only my opinion not a fact.

Life Changes

The day finally arrived in March of 1987, when Allen, Michael, and I drove Jason to his new home in Abbottstown, Pennsylvania, which was located just north of York and south of Gettysburg, Pennsylvania. We were helping Jason settle into his room. Jason met his two roommates. His room was very clean, had two windows, which created a lot of light, and it was cheerful.

The day was almost over and the dreadful time had arrived to leave our dear son and brother alone with a new family. I was watching Jason trying to read his thoughts. As we put on our coats, I looked into his eyes, and he looked at me as if to ask, "Where is my coat?" When we approached the door, I continued to watch him for his reaction. He started showing sadness in his eyes as if he was asking, "Are you leaving me here? Are you going home without me?"

My heart was breaking and tears were forming. I walked out of the room refusing to look back. I could not take the look in his eyes. It was too painful to watch. We were leaving our beloved child, and I could not stop the dreadful pain I was feeling.

We gathered ourselves in the car and left the parking lot. There were no words shared. The three of us just stared out the window of the car in silence; each dealing with our own sorrow.

As a parent, I imagined one day I would drive Michael to college and say good-bye. This was a very sad moment. One can probably use this analogy in this respect. However, Jason was only eight years old. He was not going off to college. He was going to live away from me for the rest of his life. The only analogy related to my situation is mourning. I was mourning the death of my child. The child I took care of for eight years was way too young to leave home.

We continued to sit in silence all the way home. I was emotionally spent not able to cope with my emotions, tears actually flowing from my eyes down my cheeks. I was not used to this kind of emotion. I spent too many years keeping my feelings in, and it appeared I was losing control.

After an hour of driving and self-absorbing, I realized Michael was sitting quietly in the back seat, and I turned around to check on him. He had tears in his eyes. Michael, who was only eight years old, was experiencing emotions. He was not crying because he was scolded, he was not crying because he didn't feel well, he was crying because his brother was leaving our home. He was too young to feel this kind of emotion. I quickly turned back and decided to leave him alone in his own sorrow. I wondered, "How this would affect him. Do I need to worry about the obvious trauma he was experiencing?"

We were now continuing our daily lives without Jason. To admit to ourselves our lives were less stressful was very difficult to face, but it was. I was now free to search for a job and look for suitable babysitting arrangements for Michael before and after school.

February 1987, Dad called to tell me he would like to schedule an unveiling for mom's grave stone earlier than planned because he met a woman in Florida, and wanted to marry her.

An unveiling in the Jewish faith is when the head stone for the grave is purchased and an "unveiling" service is performed. Normally, the grieved spouse and family wait at least six months for the unveiling to take place; this is out of respect for the dead, in my opinion. My dad already made the arrangements. It was only three months since mom died.

My sister and I were flabbergasted. We felt it was disrespectful to mom. However, this was what dad wanted, and we caved in and reluctantly agreed.

Dad scheduled the unveiling the day after my niece's Bat Mitzvah. He was driving up from Florida with his girlfriend to attend the Bat Mitzvah and the unveiling. I must give either my father or his girlfriend some credit. She did not attend the unveiling. Arlene and I both agreed it would not be appropriate, and apparently, Dad agreed as well.

Dad called in mid-April to invite Arlene and me to come to Florida to attend their wedding which was planned for May. We did not want to go. Our first impression of dad's girlfriend was not a good one. We were not happy and were disappointed at his behavior. Out of respect and being dutiful daughters, we flew down to Florida to attend the wedding.

Dad sold the condominium he lived in with mom and moved in with his girlfriend. The wedding took place at their condominium.

As I repeatedly made it clear, I no longer feel anything close to emotional pain. I just survived day–by–day waiting for the next problem to occur. It was a day-by-day state of living for me. With that being said, Arlene and I stood listening to the rabbi perform the ceremony. A small group of friends attended the ceremony, and Arlene and I were the only family. During the ceremony, Arlene walked away and went into the bathroom so she could be alone to express her emotion in private. It was extremely difficult for both of us to watch dad marry another woman so soon after mom's death, and Arlene was having difficulty understanding our dad's mental status and his decision making.

We were on our way home. We were scheduled to take a small commuter plane from the Palm Beach Airport to the Orlando Airport. We were then scheduled on a flight out of Orlando

Airport to Philadelphia. The commuter plane was very small, and Arlene and I never experienced flying in a small plane. We were holding hands feeling apprehensive as the plane took off. I looked out the window, and saw the clouds were very close. My mind wandered thinking about Mom, *Was she among the clouds watching over us right now?*

I shared my wandering thoughts with Arlene, and we both chuckled. However, we agreed it was comforting to know she may be watching over us.

We cannot understand why Dad didn't explain his thought process. Why did he need to remarry so quickly? We just needed him to help us understand, but he did not and that led to confusion and uncertainty. I wasn't affected by dad's decision as much as Arlene was. I was not feeling anything

Jason Adjusting to New Home

While Jason was living at home, I took him to the Children's Hospital of Philadelphia (CHOP). They had a wonderful Cerebral Palsy Clinic referred to as the CP Clinic.

Our first visit was mind-blowing. Jason and I were escorted to a room where a social worker interviewed us. She noted all of my questions and concerns. We were asked to stay in the room. What happened next astonished me, and I was not expecting it. Based on the notes the social worker took and the questions and concerns I voiced, Jason was evaluated by a speech therapist, occupational therapist, physical therapist, medical doctor, orthopedic doctor, and a nurse practitioner. We left that day exhausted but feeling like we were well taken care of.

I continued to take Jason to CHOP CP Clinic every six months until he left home. At our last visit, the orthopedic surgeon was consulted. He evaluated Jason and found his right hip needed to be repaired, and he recommended orthopedic surgery at that time.

Jason was still waiting for a bed at the Children's Developmental Center. We decided to pursue the surgery and I researched rehabilitation centers if the surgery would be performed in Philadelphia. He would need a place for post-operative care. After surgery, Jason would be in a full cast from his waist to his ankles, and I knew I could not care for him at home with this type of cast in place.

It turned out the surgery was never scheduled at CHOP because we were told a bed became available at the Children's Developmental Center and we decided to wait until he moved. This would eliminate the need for a rehabilitation center since the home had 24/7 nursing care.

A month or two after Jason moved to the Children's Developmental Center, we took him to see an orthopedic surgeon at the Elizabethtown Rehabilitation Center in Elizabethtown, Pennsylvania. This surgeon agreed with the other surgeon's findings in Philadelphia, and we scheduled Jason to have surgery on his right hip.

CP children who are spastic often develop orthopedic problems because of pressure the spasticity places on their joints. In Jason's case, it was the right hip joint that needed to be replaced.

Jason had his surgery in July of 1987. After the surgery, he was placed in a full cast from his waist to his ankles on both legs with a bar spreading the legs apart to keep the right hip immobile. I was asked to visit Jason in the recovery room. I entered the room, sat by his side, and called his name. He opened his eyes and presented me with a typical pout for which I believed meant he was scared. I did not really know how to read his expressions. I wished I was able to read his mind. I was beginning to understand some of his expressions, but I was not sure of their true meaning.

He returned to the center in a couple days. The nurses were experienced caring for him since they had other clients who underwent the same surgery. After a few days' back at his home, Jason returned to his happy self and tolerated the cast and the situation he was in. The staff at the center built a cart for their clients who had this surgery, and they placed Jason on the cart. This offered him the opportunity to get out of his bed and see his friends. You know Jason loved being on this cart because he was getting the attention he so needed.

He recovered pretty quickly, and eventually the cast was removed. He started physical therapy again to help with range of motion of for both hips and legs that were immobile while he was in the cast for two months.

New Friends and Environment

Jason quickly adjusted to his new home. I knew he missed us. I now understood very clearly this was a better place for him. He was receiving 24/7 skilled nursing care, excellent support with well-trained daily care givers. He had so many friends. He was a loving child who thrived on personal contact and attention, and he certainly got it. The more attention you gave him, the more he wanted. He quickly figured out if he smiled a lot he would get attention; he now smiled all the time!

Allen, Michael, and I saw him on a regular basis once a month. When we would enter his room and he saw us, he would be thrilled. He knew we were taking him somewhere in our car and would spend the day with him.

There were several places to take him, but most of the time we ended up at the mall, which appeared to be his favorite place of all. We either ate lunch at the mall or we would take him to a local restaurant.

The town where Jason lived was small and the people were very friendly. We started making friends with people we often saw either at the mall or at the local restaurant. We were beginning to feel part of Jason's community.

The day visiting Jason was very long. We were in the car for five hours that did not include time driving locally through the towns with Jason. It was a very long day for all of us, but we religiously visited him every month.

When Jason lived in Philadelphia and we would take him to the local mall, we found people staring at him. There were times when parents would purposely guide their children around us so they would not be near Jason. It occurred to me they may have thought their child would catch whatever disease Jason had.

In Abbottstown, this was not prevalent. People here would stop and say hello to Jason because they either knew him or they worked at the center or a family member worked there. It was a very friendly community, and people knew each other. This confirms my belief Jason belonged in this community away from the big city.

Jason had a friend whose name was also Jason. Everyone referred to him as Jason L. He moved around the center on a scooter lying on his stomach securely strapped in. He moved from room to room visiting all of his friends on the scooter. The staff soon realized Jason probably would like scooting around as well.

If you recall, in an earlier chapter, I wrote Jason scooted around the floor in our living room and wound up half-way under the couch. When I heard they were considering building a scooter for Jason, I gave them my blessing because I knew he would love it.

One day, they placed both Jason and Jason L on their scooters and off they went. I was told Jason L was faster and often would turn around to help drag Jason along. After a while, Jason learned to use his hands to help maneuver himself around better. They both wandered in and out of rooms including the nurses station.

My Career

Jason was adjusting, so it was time for me to find a full-time job. I accepted a position at the hospital where I previously worked before the boys were born. The job was a medical secretarial position in the rheumatology department. It was difficult getting back into the groove of an eight-hour work day after being away from it for eight years. When I left my previous job in 1979, I was using a state-of-the-art electric typewriter.

After working in this department for a few months, I was walking past the personnel office and saw a bulletin board on the wall with posted job listings. Among the listings, I found an intriguing job that caught my attention. It was advertised as a medical secretarial position in the neurology department. They were opening a clinic for neurologically impaired children. I thought I would be a perfect candidate for this job. I figured with all the experience I had with Jason, I would be a valuable asset for this department. I applied for the position, and I got it.

I was working at this new job for a few months. The doctor I worked for was a very high strung, unorganized, and stressed out individual. Throughout the day, she would literally throw work on my desk. She appeared to be overwhelmed starting a new clinic, and with her not being an organized individual, she was expecting me to help her organize herself along with all the various duties I was responsible for. Unfortunately, I was the only support person running the front desk. I was expected to help her and perform my responsibilities as well. We were not getting along. We had two entirely different types of personalities, and I found myself not enjoying working with someone who was very hyper and unorganized. She was stressing me out, and I was having difficulty working under these conditions.

I worked in the past in difficult situations and eventually everything worked out; why can't I do it now? Taking care of the boys for eight years taught me how to multitask. "Why am I having difficulty with this job and dealing with this doctor?" I constantly asked myself.

After a few more months, it finally occurred to me the true reason I was not comfortable with this job, and it wasn't the personality conflict with the doctor. I realized I was affected by the children at the clinic who were being treated. Many of the children were Jason's age and had cerebral palsy, but they were walking with crutches and they were capable of speaking. It was affecting me emotionally and affecting my ability to do my job at the level I knew I could.

One day, early in the morning before the clinic opened, my boss and I sat down to chat. She told me she felt the job was too much for me to handle.

"No, it isn't the job or even you, I think it is affecting my emotions having contact with children treated in this clinic on a daily basis," I replied.

She thought about what I said and responded, "You just may be right about that. Maybe working in the medical field is no longer a good setting for you. You dealt with your boys and your mother for the past eight years. You probably need to work in an entirely different environment for you to succeed. You are an excellent worker, and I know you will find the right job outside the medical field you can build a future with."

I thanked her for her understanding, and we ended the chat agreeing I would leave the job.

Again I was unemployed. My past working history included working in the cardiology department for ten years before I became pregnant. I was always proud with the fact I could stay at a job for a long stretch. I am not the same person I was back in 1979. I needed to find a job that suited the new me.

I decided to take a different route and applied for a government position. Both my parents were government employees, and they loved working at their jobs. It can provide good benefits and security.

Four months after applying for a government job, I was asked to come in for an interview. The job was advertised as an administrative assistant for the Northeast Regional Office of the Bureau of Prisons. The Bureau of Prisons was located in the Customs House in the historic district of downtown Philadelphia.

I interviewed for the job early on a Monday morning, and I received a phone call that afternoon offering me the job. I was shocked and very flattered. After the experience I had at the hospital, I lost confidence in myself and my abilities. I apparently made an impression. I didn't immediately say yes because the salary range for this grade level in a government position was much less than what I made at the hospital I needed to think it through.

After discussing the pros and cons with Allen that evening, I decided to take the job. The benefits this government job offered eventually outweighed my pay cut and there was an opportunity for advancement as well. Since my parents both had government jobs, I knew it would be a benefit to me because they offered a good vacation and sick pay. This definitely sealed the deal since I could accrue time quickly to allow me to attend meetings and doctor appointments with Jason. I called the next day and accepted the job.

I enjoyed this job, and I slowly transitioned myself as a government employee. I found it to be a much slower pace than my previous position as a medical secretary. It would take some adjustment to get used to the pace. I did find myself much more relaxed working without the stress I did in the previous job.

After working eight months in the department I was hired for, I was approached by the comptroller in the financial management department. He heard "through the grapevine" that I was asking about a job he listed and placed on the bulletin board. He told me to apply for it and then walked away. This took me by surprise.

Earlier that week, I found the job listing on the bulletin board. The job was at a higher grade level then what I was. It was described to be a financial assistant position working directly under the comptroller of the department. The description listed on the announcement intrigued me. I commented to my friend who joined me for lunch, "Did you see the job listed on the bulletin board for a financial assistant in the financial management department? This job sounds intriguing and I just may apply for it."

I was taken back somewhat. Boy, word really flies in this small office. However, I was flattered that he approached me, and it appeared he was hinting to me to apply, so I did and I got the job.

The comptroller who coaxed me and hired me for the job left the Regional Office two months later. A new comptroller took over a month after he left.

In the meantime, because of the transitioning of comptrollers in our department, the training for my position was nonexistent. I was learning my new job by trial and error. The new comptroller, George, was not aware of this fact, and I didn't tell him. After we had a few clashes in our personalities with differences and misunderstandings, I told him, and we eventually worked it out. It turned out we became good friends, colleagues, and he served to be someone I was able to count on for support through the years. He saw me as someone he could count on as well to trust explicitly and back him when he needed to make necessary changes throughout the years to help support his position as the comptroller of the Northeast Regional Office. In return, I received the support I needed for me to continue to advocate for Jason's needs and be with Jason when it was necessary.

Working for the Bureau of Prisons Regional Office was the best decision I made. I met many good people and good friends. I do not know what I would have done without the support and comfort I received from all my coworkers throughout the years.

Lincoln Intermediate Center

Jason started school in September after arriving at the Children's Intermediate Center the previous February. He was going to the Lincoln Intermediate Center in York, which was a thirty-minute bus trip one way. As in Philadelphia, he was placed in a severely profoundly impaired classroom in a regular elementary school. I was told Jason loved getting dressed and secured in his wheelchair each morning and waited eagerly in line with the other children for the school bus to arrive. He was happy because he knew he would be placed on the lift, and if you remember, he loved the lift and considered it his own personal amusement ride. What a character!

Jason's classroom consisted of one teacher and two aides, appropriately staffed based on his IEP. Earlier in this book, I described an IEP, which was an Individual Educational Plan set up to document Jason's goals and objectives and was renewed periodically.

At our first IEP meeting, I met Jason's teacher and the two aides who were assigned to his room. My first impression of Jason's teacher, whose name was Meladye, was an intelligent and compassionate woman. After Jason's IEP meeting, I watched her with her students and was very impressed with her ability to communicate with each child and give each child individual attention.

I predicted Jason would love her immediately. She was a beautiful woman with long blonde hair, and Jason was a sucker for beautiful women. My prediction was correct. Jason started his flirting techniques, and Meladye took to it immediately. Jason had long eyelashes and beautiful big eyes, and he used his attributes successfully to gain attention. Meladye fell under his spell.

Meladye was Jason's teacher for a few years and Allen, Michael, and I developed a wonderful relationship with her and her husband. We often talked on the phone and she would send letters reporting Jason's progress in quarterly reports. On November 15, 1990, her note stated the following: "As always Jason is such a joy to work with. He continues to be a very happy and hardworking student as well as a special friend."

An additional report stated, "He would use the yes and no board 95% with verbal prompting and would choose desirable positions on a communication board 83% with verbal prompting. In motor skills he would operate a variety of switches 96% of the time and reach for and grasp objects 100% of the time. He would tolerate sitting in a feeder seat for 45 minutes." She ended this note to say, "Jason is continuing to grow and learn and he loves to work!"

Because I knew Jason so well, I knew he would do anything she asked him to do just to get her attention and have the opportunity to flirt. She was aware of his flirting, and it only encouraged her to work harder with him.

Occasionally, I would take a day off from work and visit Jason at school. During one of my visits, Meladye commented I was not communicating with Jason correctly. She told me I was talking at him, rather than directly to him, and I just may have the opportunity to understand his needs if I could learn how to communicate correctly.

"Here let me show you what I am talking about." She asked me to sit directly in front of him and look into his eyes. As I was looking into his eyes, she told me to ask him a question and I would hear an answer. I am not clear what I was looking for. However, after I started asking Jason questions I knew would require a response, I finally understood. I received my answer with eye contact, a smile, pout, frown, or just a simple facial expression. I knew a few of his expression already because I understood what his pout meant. However, this took it one step further helping me to understand and communicate with Jason. This validated my belief Jason was not mentally retarded. He could communicate. He knew what I was asking him to do and what I was saying to him. I needed to learn how to listen to his response. He was compensating for what he could not do.

"I am feeling shame for not realizing this myself," I told her.

"It is an acquired process understanding how to communicate with Jason. This is a learned skill only a qualified professional can show you."

I was so blessed! What an amazing teacher!

From that time forward, I could communicate with Jason looking directly into his eyes. He would smile, frown, or use facial expressions in response. I now had a connection to my son I never had before. I saw my son as an intelligent child who had needs and he now could communicate these needs to me. We were not only communicating we were connecting spiritually as well. This was when spirituality entered my life. I understand the gift I was given and what I needed to do in order to continue to give Jason the love and support he needed.

Through the years, Meladye and I often communicated through letters and phone conversations. She invited Jason to her home a few times for weekend visits, and Jason loved the time he spent with her.

In another letter, she said, "Jason is, as always, such a joy to have in my classroom and my life. He is always so pleasant, even when he had a high fever, he smiled! He can always bring a smile to my face and everyone else he touches."

In another letter, she stated, "He is working hard to identify colors and classmates and at times, his family. He appears to miss you and longs for you. I think the pictures I show of his family and especially you, set off memories. Jason loves art, music, gym, and speech and has been doing very well in each of these. Jason is very near and dear to my heart, and I love having his smiling face and pleasant attitude and special friendship!"

Jason Meets Doctor Segal

After Jason's surgery at Elizabeth Rehabilitation Center, the hospital merged with Hershey Medical Center. Jason was referred to an orthopedic surgeon, Dr. Segal at Hershey Medical Center. I scheduled an appointment for Jason to be examined by him.

I drove from Philadelphia to meet Jason for his first visit with Dr. Segal. Jason and I were waiting in the examining room when he entered. He immediately approached Jason, said hello, and asked him how he was. He looked directly into his eyes as he talked to him. Jason just sat in his wheelchair checking him out. I knew Jason. If he didn't like him he would pout and moan as if to say, "Take me out of here." For many reasons, Jason did not like hospitals. Because Dr. Segal approached Jason first before directing his attention to me, showed me he respected Jason and would treat him with the dignity he deserved. I liked this doctor!

He examined him moving his limbs slowly and methodically so as not to hurt him. After the examination, Dr. Segal reached for the X-ray that was taken earlier and placed it on the light board hanging on the wall. He looked at me and pointed at the X-ray and said, "This is his left hip joint, and it shows definite deterioration at the joint. It is my recommendation he should have this corrected, and I also suggest performing bilateral knee tendon strengthening to help give him more range of motion in the back of his knees."

"Okay, we are now facing another surgery, Jason," I related as I started dressing him and placed him back in his wheelchair after Dr. Segal left the room. I walked out to the hallway and found Dr. Segal at a desk writing notes. I approached him and said, "Okay, schedule the surgery. As you know, his right hip was corrected over a year ago, and I was told at that time his left hip was showing signs of deterioration. I anticipated your findings and prepared myself for Jason's second orthopedic surgical procedure."

Two months passed since the initial appointment with Dr. Segal and the surgery was scheduled by Dr. Segal at Hershey Medical Center. Allen had a work commitment that he needed to take care of but he was planning on driving up after work with Michael. We had reservations to stay at the Hershey Lodge across the street from the hospital. Meladye offered to spend the day waiting with me knowing I would be alone.

We both helped Jason undress and ready for the nurses to prep him for surgery. We were asked to go with Jason to the pre-op room. Our presence would keep him calm. You could see his facial expression was showing an attitude he was not happy. He was older and was becoming much more aware of where he was and what was going to happen to him. I looked at him and asked him how he was. He looked back at me with a pout as if to say, "Take me away from here. I don't want another surgery." I was trying to provide comfort and so was Meladye, but we were both scared as well,

Dr. Segal approached Jason's bed and shook his hand and told him everything was going to be all right. He told him he was going to make him feel better and will do his best to rid Jason of the pain he was having in his hip and the back of his knees. Dr. Segal then turned to both Meladye and myself and asked us, "Do you know Jason is not retarded?"

I was somewhat surprised at his question not expecting it at this time. However, I quickly responded to him and said, "Yes, I know he isn't retarded." He then walked away with a smile on his face.

Of course, we both knew Jason wasn't retarded. We were sitting in the surgical waiting room and shared out thoughts about his surprising question.

"This is the first time since Jason's birth that any doctor took the time to ask me this question or offer their opinion. I am surprised and very impressed at the same time. I really like this doctor. He certainly shows a lot of compassion and respect for children like Jason," I said.

She agreed with me 100 percent and said, "I never met a doctor like him, and I had many experiences with professionals in my career. He is one hell of a doctor."

"I agree."

It was four hours later, and we were still sitting in the waiting room when Dr. Segal finally arrived in his OR scrubs. He obviously came directly to see me after completing Jason's surgery.

"Jason tolerated the surgery very well, and you are welcome to see him in the recovery room," he told me. "I believe it will benefit Jason to see both of you when he awakes from the anesthesia. He will be scared. Jason will tell you he is in pain and you can ask the nurse to give him medicine."

When we arrived in the recovery room Jason was already awake. As I approached him I found the typical pout and tears in his eyes. I asked him if he was in pain, and he pouted again. I told the nurse he was in pain and please give him pain medicine. She did and he fell back to sleep soon after. My communications skills were working!

He was transferred to his hospital room, and we sat with him for a while. Allen and Michael arrived an hour later. Meladye excused herself and left for home. We all stayed with Jason for a little while longer and then left to get something to eat.

Jason was in the same cast he had with the previous surgery. It extended from his waist down to his ankles on both legs with a bar separating his legs. It looked so uncomfortable, but Jason was a trooper, and as long as I continued to request pain medicine when he asked me for it, he was calm and slept quietly. We all stayed by his side for the remaining hospital stay until he was discharged.

He returned back to the center in an ambulance, and as the previous surgery, the nurses were prepared and ready to care for his needs.

B'Nai Mitzvah

We entered a new decade, the 1990s. Every time we visited Jason, he recognized me and Allen and Michael. He even remembered our extended family as well. I was so relieved to know he hasn't forgotten us. I continued to be amazed with every visit learning so much about his intelligence and his ability to reach out to others. He continued to find a way to express himself with facial expressions to show his approval, happiness, sadness, and so many other emotions.

One day, I received a special gift in the mail from Jason. He made it in school and Meladye sent it to me. I opened the package and read the note and I simply was astonished. I placed it in a special place in my house where I could see it all the time. It was a simple block of wood that was wrapped with a cloth and a simple bow. There was a note on top of the gift which read,

> This is a very special gift that you can never see. The reason it's so special is it's just for you from me. Whenever you are lonely or even feeling blue, you only have to hold this gift and know I think of you. You never should unwrap it, please leave the ribbon tied. Hold the box close to your heart; it's filled with love inside. Love Jason.

Oh my god. I will never ever receive a gift this special for the rest of my life. This gift serves as a reminder that everything I did for my son to make his life worthwhile was worth it.

On June 20, 1992 Jason and Michael became men in the eyes of the Jewish faith.

In the Jewish religion, when a boy or a girl turns thirteen, they are considered to be a man/woman, and the boy will have a Bar Mitzvah and a girl would have a Bat Mitzvah. However, in our case since they were twins, it was referred to as a B'nai Mitzvah.

We were lucky. We found a wonderful tutor to help Michael learn the Torah reading in order for him to perform his part at his Bar Mitzvah. She was a student at the Rabbinical Society in Philadelphia, and she tutored Michael twice a week.

Typically, a young boy would start Hebrew school at the age of eight and would have five years of training to prepare him for the special day. We felt if Michael would attend both regular school and Hebrew school three days a week for three hours, it would be too much of a burden for him. He was doing so well in special education we didn't want to add further pressure to his schedule.

It was now June 20, 1992, and the day finally arrived. We picked Jason up on Thursday. We had an appointment with the photographer to take the still family pictures and single pictures of both Michael and Jason on Friday. The photographer we found had experience working with special needs children, and he assured us he would get good pictures of Jason.

We were having a twilight service on Saturday night with a cocktail hour immediately following the service. We carefully planned everything out so that it would be convenient for us and our guest. We chose a local hotel as the venue for the entire affair. We were given a room in case Jason needed to leave the reception early.

Originally, we planned to hire a nurse to take care of Jason for the evening. However, after talking to Meladye earlier in the month, she insisted we not hire a nurse. She said she would care for Jason.

"We invited you to attend the B'nai Mitzvah as a guest, not a nurse," I explained carefully to her. I wanted her and her husband to enjoy themselves and not have to care for Jason.

"Oh no, Mrs. Quate, it will be my honor to care for Jason. I plan on enjoying the entire evening and taking care of Jason will not keep me from doing so. It is my pleasure to care for him," she responded most precisely. She certainly was clear in her intent and I gave in to her request.

My father arrived from Florida with his wife. My relationship with my father was deteriorating. I was still very resentful, and it was affecting me more than I thought it would.

After meeting my father's wife, I did not like her. She was very self-centered. I was usually open to most people's idiocies and would be cordial to such a person but will usually not extend a friendship to them.

The years since my mom's death and dad's remarriage, dad and his wife would visit in the summer for a few weeks. My dad still had his house in Philadelphia. When they came to Philadelphia, Dad did not see Jason. I did not understand the change in his personality and his feelings toward Jason. He absolutely loved Jason, and he never backed away from holding him, babysitting for him, or playing and interacting with Jason. He was supportive in so many ways, I was upset with him and did not understand his changes since my mom died.

I later learned dad's wife did not want to visit Jason. She was unable to be in the presence of a person with Jason's disabilities. I did say she was self-centered! Therefore, because of her self-centered attitude, dad chose to take her side and he did not visit Jason. He related to Arlene one day he didn't want to leave his wife alone. The tension was building and eventually had reached the boiling point.

It had been a long time since Jason visited us. I was no longer in the mode of caring for him 24/7. Having him home again proved to be very difficult. There was so much to prepare for and caring for Jason at home just added to the tension.

We left for the hotel earlier in the day so we would have enough time to dress. I was having difficulty dressing Jason. I couldn't get his suit jacket on because the spasticity in his upper joints increased and the more I tried to get his arm through the jacket sleeve, the more spastic he became. I was now in tears because I couldn't get his jacket on, and we needed to be downstairs to greet out guests.

I stopped maneuvering his arm and held Jason in my arms. It occurred to me he was feeling my tension and was reacting to it. I started to lightly rub his arms and rock him slightly, and I took a few deep breaths. Jason started to respond, and I asked Allen to very slowly move his loosened arm into his jacket sleeve while I was holding him. We readjusted him slightly and managed to place his other arm through the sleeve. We did it! Jason smiled! Allen adjusted Jason's tie. We both placed him in his wheelchair. We headed out the door and walked toward the elevator hoping we weren't too late.

I started the service with a speech I prepared.

> Welcome to Michael and Jason's B'nai Mitzvah. We are very proud of both of our sons today and so pleased that you all can share this moment with us.
>
> Our hearts are filled with love and joy for our son Michael who developed into a fine person. Today as we watch him enter a new phase of his life, we are so thankful for the miracle that brought him to us, and we wish him a life filled with health and happiness.
>
> Today, we will also witness a very special moment when Jason experiences his Bar Mitzvah. We believe in our hearts Jason understands the importance of this day. We only pray that Jason will accept the love that we all give

him and with it he gains the strength to endure what life will continue to bring him.

Today, as Michael recites his Bar Mitzvah service he will form a union with his brother, and together, they will experience their B'nai Mitzvah. The love that they share as brothers will give Michael the support and courage to stand before you as a Bar Mitzvah boy. We would like to thank you for being part of our sons' special day.

The service was over and let the party begin!

Traditionally, as part of the celebration, a candle lighting service takes place. Family and friends, who were chosen to be part of the candle lighting service, were called up to light a candle and congratulate the family with hugs and kisses.

When it was my father and his wife's turn to light a candle, my father hugged and kissed all of us. However, my father's wife hugged and kissed everyone but Jason and quickly returned to her seat. I was not aware what she did until later on in the evening. Apparently, it was not unnoticed among some of our friends and family. They were appalled at her behavior.

When I saw the video a few weeks later I was also appalled at her obvious discrimination she presented to Jason in front of my friends and family. This was when I decided I no longer wanted to have anything to do with her. This caused more strain in the relationship between my father and me.

Jason Experiencing Difficulties

Jason was beginning to have seizures, according to the nurses at the center. The doctor at the center had all of Jason's previous hospital records way back to 1979 when he was born. The records revealed Jason experienced seizures while he was in the NICU, and he was given medicine for controlling them.

Allen and I forgot or we were not informed he was having seizures at that time. In addition, during the eight years Jason lived at home, we never saw him have a seizure. I now understand there are many forms of seizures, one of which could manifest as a staring-like state. During the years he was home with us, I probably would not have been alarmed because Jason would often sit in his chair and stare. I didn't see his staring as a problem or a seizure. I may have thought he was just thinking about something and was sitting quietly.

However, the nurses were experienced in recognizing seizures and knew what to look for and they started charting his episodes.

An appointment was scheduled with a neurologist at Hershey Medical Center, and I attended as well. The doctor explained to me, "The EEG is not clear enough to identify a seizure activity but it shows some abnormal lines." He continued, "These abnormal lines usually are seen in EEGs in cerebral palsy victims but there is no significant relationship related to a seizure. I suggest Jason be placed on a seizure medicine because the history the nurses have noted in their charting are significant enough for me to warrant prescribing a mild seizure medicine."

I was beginning to worry about the signs of deterioration in Jason. He was now having seizures and was diagnosed with a gastrointestinal reflux five months after birth. He was now experiencing more difficulty controlling the condition and it was now considered a disease.

The Gastroesophageal Reflux disease (GERD) is a chronic digestive disease that occurs when stomach acid or, occasionally, bile flows back (refluxes) into your food pipe (esophagus). The backwash of acid irritates the lining of your esophagus and causes GERD signs and symptoms. Jason started vomiting about one-half hour or less after meals. At first, it was occasionally, and now, it was occurring more often.

The nurses along with the dietician arranged a meeting to troubleshoot and make a decision. I attended the meeting also. I was sitting around a table with a nurse, dietician, head nurse, and an aide. Prior to this meeting, Jason was evaluated at the feeding clinic at York General Hospital, and they indicated Jason's swallowing was slowly deteriorating due to his reflux. The report strongly recommended, due to a very high risk of aspiration, he have a feeding tube placed.

I had a feeling this was being presented today, but I certainly was hoping it would not be necessary. My son may now lose the ability to taste food. What more?

The person who feeds him has been thickening his foods, feeding him slower, and giving him thickened liquids, but he was still coughing up particles of his food, which was not a good sign. She told us, "I feed Jason, and I am getting increasingly concerned because he is coughing every time he swallows, sometimes with really bad spasms that scare me. I am afraid he is going to aspirate."

I was sitting and listening very carefully trying to absorb the information being reported.

The dietician showed me a chart she was keeping noting his food intake, calories, and the amount of food intake related to his weight. She was looking directly at me, so I can clearly understand the importance of what she was saying. "Mrs. Quate, in the past month, he lost six pounds, and I believe this weight loss represents him not getting enough food and nourishment. He is vomiting almost everything he is fed. He has a very strong risk of aspirating that could cause aspirating pneumonia."

The meeting ending with all the people in attendance agreeing Jason should have a feeding tube placed.

I must have had a scared look on my face because the dietician took my hand and said, "Please do not be upset. Most of the clients here who have difficulty like Jason have a feeding tube, and they are thriving and gaining weight." She began to describe what it would consist of and explained to me that "the gastroenterologist will cut a small hole near his belly button and will insert, what is called, a button. It looks like a plug. I will prescribe a special nutritious diet in a liquid form fed directly into his stomach, bypassing the esophagus, through a tube connected to the button. I will closely monitor his intake to include the proper nourishment and calories based on Jason's height and weight. He should show a weight gain immediately."

After listening to all the professionals and their evaluations, I agreed and asked them to schedule the appointment for the doctor to insert the button.

I drove home trying to process all of what I heard that day. I was concerned about my child and how he appeared to be deteriorating. He was sixteen years old now. For the first time since birth, I was again thinking about his life span. In the past few years, he started with seizures and getting medicine now to control them. Now, he will lose the ability to taste food, and he will be fed through a tube and his spasticity was increasing.

In addition, at the recent visit with Dr. Segal, he told me Jason was developing a curvature of his spine, and he measured it to be thirty-five degrees. He told me if or when it reached sixty degrees he would seriously consider performing a spinal fusion. He will insert a rod into his spine to straighten the curvature. This was consistent with an individual who has spastic cerebral palsy, and it usually develops at they get older.

How do I comprehend all of this?

We as parents want to protect our children from being hurt. We want them to be healthy and vibrant. I never had guarantees, but did have hope and now the hope was beginning to extinguish itself from my being. I suppose I needed to leave it up to god and his will to take over. He gave Jason to me, and I suppose he will take him back when he is ready.

Since Jason is still with us I need to be brave and watch him suffer through pain and discomfort in his joints, deterioration of his body, and the ordeal of further surgical procedures. The only positive signs I saw was his pleasant personality and beautiful smile. He would never show me any signs of pain even though I knew he suffered from a lot of pain. He had both hips replaced and the muscles in the back of his knees stretched. His spasticity must be painful. He loved me and want to hide his pain from me. He knew I loved when he smiled and that was what was most important to him, making me happy.

The decision was made to place the feeding tube because the worse scenario wasn't worth the risk. With Jason's respiratory difficulties, if he developed aspirating pneumonia, it would be very difficult for him to recover from it.

Jason was only required to stay overnight at York General Hospital, and I decided not to go because of my work commitments. I did receive a phone call immediately after the procedure from the gastroenterologist who assured me Jason tolerated it well.

It took time to adjust the feeding process to assure the best results for Jason. It required trying different sources. For example, a bolus feeding defined as simply pouring the liquid quickly through the tube or a slow drip. A slow drip was similar to an IV where one could adjust how many drips per minutes. The decision was based on how Jason responded.

It appeared the bolus feeding was not working because he was still vomiting after feedings. However, the slow drip proved to work the best. Jason stopped vomiting.

We are now faced with a decision. Because of the problem Jason exhibited with his feeding, he was kept home from school for a few months.

Another meeting was arranged to discuss the possibility of Jason attending the homebound school at the center. I did not attend the meeting. Edith, Jason's longtime social worker following his case, called me and we discussed the probability of his attending the homebound class at the center. She reported the results of their discussion at the meeting. All staff involved with Jason who attended the meeting felt he should begin homebound classes. She read me the notes she took during the meeting and how they came to the conclusion. The nurses felt very strongly now that Jason receives his feeding through a slow drip, it would be to Jason's best interest not to travel on the bus. In addition, the school does not have a full-time nurse who could monitor the feeding on a regular basis throughout the school day. Many problems could occur with clogging of the tubes, which will require immediate attention.

Reluctantly, I agreed. I drove up from Philadelphia to meet the homebound teacher and his aide. I was impressed with the classroom and the ability to continue the quality of education Jason had been receiving at the Lincoln Intermediate Center.

I was upset. This was the end of a beautiful relationship with a great and loving teacher Jason had the privilege to have for several years. Meladye and I talked on the phone, and she understood and agreed we made the right decision for Jason. I could hear and feel the sadness she expressed. She grew to love Jason, and I knew she wanted to continue working with him and help him reach his greatest potential. However, this was something we both needed to accept. I reminded her she could visit Jason any time she wanted and she agreed to do so.

Jason's Personality

A long time ago, I accepted the label society placed on Jason, mental retardation. I understood because Jason was severely physically disabled that affected his ability to learn. On the positive side, he was entitled to many services for which Allen and I would not be able to provide. The cost would be astronomical. I made myself very clear several times through this book how I felt. I accepted it, and I am not ashamed.

There were times when Jason was able to show us what he could understand. He managed to find a way to express his abilities that astonished both Allen and I and his personal staff at the center. Here are a few examples of how Jason expressed himself in different situations.

I was with Jason and a staff member at a routine appointment with Dr. Segal. Dr. Segal was unusually late with an emergency. He never was late before. Jason and Dr. Segal had a great relationship. Normally, Jason was very patient and would wait in his chair quietly for a long time. On this day and because he was over an hour late, Jason appeared to be anxious and tired of waiting for him.

Around two hours later, he walked into the room looking somewhat frazzled and out of sorts. He immediately approached Jason and apologized to him and then turned to us and also apologized. "There was a severe car accident with injuries that required my immediate attention. I am so sorry to keep you all waiting." He looked down at Jason and repeated, "Please forgive me. I know it is hard for you to wait so long."

I was not looking at Jason at that time, but Kim poked me to get my attention so I can see what Jason was doing. Jason's right palm was lying on his table face up. His middle finger was pointed directly at Dr. Segal.

Dr. Segal saw Jason's rude gesture, smiled, and looked at him. "I suppose I deserved that and good for you to express your feelings."

We all had a good laugh including Jason. Kim told me later a staff member taught Jason how to express his feelings and showed him how to extend his middle finger when he was angry. This certainly proved Jason can show emotion. Since he could not verbalize his emotion, this was the next best way for him to express himself. As his mother, I should have disciplined him for his vulgar gesture; instead, I was beaming with pride.

On another day, Jason was in the center's van traveling to Hershey Medical Center for an appointment. He was sitting toward the rear of the van secured in his wheelchair. There was an attachment on his wheelchair placed there by his speech therapist. It was a device he could use to express his needs. This was a goal they were working on at the time. All he needed to do was press one of the buttons. One button had a recording that said, "I am thirsty please give me a drink." Another one said, "Please get me out of my chair," and the third button said, "Hi, my name is Jason." She also attached a recorder to change the verbal recordings when needed.

The travel time from Abbottstown to Hershey was over an hour. Jason was the only passenger that day. Kim and another staff member were in the front seat with Kim driving. They were having a normal conversation just passing the time until they arrived at the hospital. After a half hour, they both were quiet when they suddenly heard their voices. She turned around and watched Jason maneuver the buttons with a big smile on his face.

Jason recorded their voices and waited until they were quiet to play it back to them. He was cracking up with "spastic spasms" showing how proud he was with himself.

When Kim told me this, at first I did not believe her. It would take a great deal of cognitive skills and physical movement for Jason to know what button to push, to record a voice, and turn it on at a specific time while they were talking. In addition, he needed to manipulate his hands in order to do this just at the right time to get the recording and then turn it on when they stopped talking so they could hear it. It would take a lot of concentration for him to know what he wanted to do and then get his brain to move his hands and fingers to actually do the chore.

There are no words to express how much I loved my child. He had a need to prove he had a functioning brain. It was extremely hard for his brain to communicate to his body to move a finger, hand, or arm. However, he did it!

There is one more story I would like to tell you. We were visiting Jason during the holiday season. We bought him a bear from Build a Bear Workshop located at our local mall. I picked out the design and clothes, and I also recorded a message so he could hear my voice whenever he wanted.

I showed Jason what he needed to do to hear my voice by pressing the bear's paw.

We were sitting in the visitors lounge and watching a football game. I was watching him maneuver the bear with some difficulty so he could reach his paw. After several minutes, he found the correct paw, squeezed it, and heard my voice. You had to see the expression of pride and astonishment on his face. He knew what he wanted, worked his brain to move his hands in order to get his hand around the paw that had the recording device, and then worked his brain to allow his hand to squeeze the paw. He did it!

Allen and I just looked at him, and we both hugged him to show how proud we were and of course he squealed with joy.

I always believed Jason was special in so many ways, and I needed to be patient with him to show me. He had the ability to understand, and he learned how to compensate in order for him to make his body do what he wanted it to do. This was not an easy chore. It took a lot of skill and concentration for him to make his brain communicate with his body to move. *Wow.* He never ceased to amaze me.

Dad's Sudden Death

Jason turned seventeen on September 8, 1996. His social calendar was full participating in boy scouts, outside trips with his friends and staff members. We continued to visit him monthly. However, now that Michael was seventeen as well, his working schedule and social activity usually stopped him from visiting Jason. I attended doctor appointments and meetings at the center.

My relationship with my father was still complicated. I did not call him, and he had not called me either. I was extremely upset over the entire situation, and it appeared it would explode into an undesirable scene if one of us did not make a move to correct the problem.

I decided to write a letter. I have difficulty dealing with confrontations, especially with family members. Writing was easier for me so that is what I did. I wrote a long letter spilling all of my pent-up feelings about his wife, her attitude toward Jason, and the issue with him not visiting Jason. He had not seen Jason since the B'nai Mitzvah, which was four years ago. I reminded him about all the good times he had with both boys and how he played and showed so much love to Jason. I also reminded him about all the support he provided through the years and how much I appreciated it. I told him I could not have survived without his and mom's support through the earlier years. Just knowing he was there backing me, helped me survive the difficult years. I ended the letter saying ever since Mom died and he remarried, he was not the same man and father. Jason no longer existed in his life. I told him I was devastated with his behavior. I knew the letter was very strong, but I felt he needed to know how I felt.

It had been several months since I mailed the letter to my dad. He did not call me.

A few weeks later, Dad called my sister Arlene and told her he was very angry with me and found my letter to be a pinnacle point in our relationship, and he no longer wanted me in his life. He was closing the door and throwing away the key!

Arlene was extremely upset and begged me, "Please, Judy, the ball is now in your court. Do you want him to die without reconciling? You will never forgive yourself. You better call him or you will regret it for the rest of your life."

"I knew she was right. I would never forgive myself. However, I was so upset with him. We apparently had the same stubborn streak—father and daughter. Someone had to give in."

I was sitting in my bedroom after I ended the conversation with Arlene and all these thoughts were going through my head. I started to cry. "Why am I crying? I never cry." I started shaking and crying so hard Allen walked into the room and reemphasized Arlene's points and told me to call him. I had no idea why but I called my mother-in-law instead. I needed a mother figure. In fifteen minutes, she was at our door. She picked up the phone while holding my hand and ordered me to call him.

I dialed his number and waited for someone to answer, hoping it was not my father's wife.

"Hello?" Dad said.

"Hi, Dad," I responded. "I am calling you. Arlene relayed your message to me."

"Oh, she did," he coldly replied.

"Dad, I had to write you the letter. It is very hard for me to face you, and I found it easier in the letter."

"I was devastated when I read it. My wife is very upset, and after she read the letter, she tore it in many pieces. She strongly urged me not to contact you because of how much you hurt her."

I made the wise choice not to respond to that statement and continued to say, "I am sorry I made you upset. I called to tell you I love you and always will."

He didn't return the sediment but did say, "I appreciate you calling me. I will see you soon. We will be driving up to Philly in a few weeks."

We both ended the call.

They arrived in Philadelphia a few weeks later. We were cordial with each other and acted like nothing happened between us. The night before they were ready to return to Florida, I invited both of them for dinner at my house and very surprisingly, we all had a great time. Apparently, all was well again. It does did not change my attitude toward his wife but I somehow found a way to deal with her and still love my dad.

After they left our house and we said our good-byes, I began to wonder what my father said to his wife to convince her to be cordial. I am wondering what their real relationship was. I could not picture my father accepting demands from his wife like she did with my letter. My mom had too much love and respect for my father to ever speak to him in that way. They had their disagreements but never were they disrespectful to each other.

We were enjoying the northeastern fall, accepting the cold winter, and the starting of spring. Jason was doing as well as expected. His feeding button needed to be replaced a few times.

Dad came down with a bad cold in early April. Every time I talked to him, he sounded so congested and was coughing very often and hard making it difficult for him to speak. He told me he was under the care of a doctor, and he gave him medicine for the bad cough.

A few days later, Dad called me back, and he very abruptly told me he had lung cancer. He told Arlene and me he was diagnosed several weeks ago, and he didn't want to worry us.

I was in shock, and I told him, "Arlene and I will come down to Florida."

He responded very sharply, making it very clear, "I do not want you to come!"

I ended the conversation. I was feeling very uneasy. "Why is he so adamant? What is going on? He is being very evasive, clearly trying to keep us from seeing him."

This conversation took place on Wednesday and the following Sunday morning, I received a call from his wife. "Your dad just collapsed and is unconscious on the floor. What should I do?"

"Hang up the phone and call 911!" I responded abruptly..

I started shaking all over. *How stupid is she?* I thought..

I returned the call fifteen minutes later, and she answered.

"What is happening? Where is my dad now?" I asked.

I didn't need an answer because I could hear the paramedics treating dad. I heard the paramedics taking care of my father. I heard one man say, "The heart is now in normal rhythm. He responded to the CPR. The IV is in place and the oxygen is working. Let me help you get him up and on the gurney." *Did I just hear they resuscitated my dad through this phone?*

"What hospital are they taking him to?" I asked her, and she told me.

I immediately hung the phone up and called Arlene. We decided to wait until dad arrived in the emergency ward and the doctor had a chance to see him before we called the hospital.

A half hour later, which felt more like an entire day, Arlene spoke to the doctor directly who was treating dad in the emergency room. He told her, "You need to come down as soon as possible because your father is in critical condition. Your father's heart stopped and the paramedics revived him."

I immediately called the airlines and booked us both on the next flight down to West Palm Beach.

Our flight left Philadelphia International Airport at 8:00 p.m. that evening. We arrived in West Palm Beach at 10:00 p.m. We immediately rented a car and drove directly to the hospital. Arlene knew what floor and room he was in. We walked out of the elevator and down the hallway toward his room when a nurse approached us and asked, "Are you Mr. Lax's daughters?"

"Yes, we are," we responded hesitantly. "What is wrong?

"Your dad went into cardiac arrest a few hours ago. He was revived and was transferred to the intensive care unit. Please let me take you to him."

We found our dad in the intensive care unit and on a respirator. He was lying very still with tubes and wires draped across his body.

"Dad, we are here," we both said.

He opened his eyes and saw us. He started to cry, and we both took one of his hands. We told him we loved him. Through the tear-filled eyes, we felt the emotional response.

"Thank you for coming. I love you both." He squeezed our hands like he was saying good-bye.

We stayed with dad for a while longer when the nurse approached. She wanted dad to get rest. She helped us find a nearby hotel, and we left the hospital. It was already the next day.

We arrived in our room and started unpacking when the phone rang. We both looked at each other and knew who it was. I answered the phone.

"Your dad passed away a few minutes ago. I am so sorry."

Our dad is now with mom and they are both at peace.

We arranged a small funeral in Florida for his friends and his wife. We arranged for dad to return to Philadelphia to be buried next to mom. This was clearly stated in a letter he left with a friend who we immediately called. Dad once told both of us if anything should happen to him, all we needed to do was call his friend and everything would be arranged.

The funeral in Philadelphia was very touching. All of his friends showed up at the funeral pallor and the grave site. He had a military funeral since he was a World War II veteran. Two army soldiers arrived from nearby Fort Dix Army Base, and they provided the military ceremony playing taps, had a gun salute and the ritual of folding the American flag and presenting it to Arlene and me. It was a wonderful tribute to my father, and I will never forget it. I am at peace because Mom and Dad are now together again for eternity.

Spinal Fusion/Baclofen Pump

It was now 1998, and Jason was nineteen years old. He continued to attend the home bound school at the center where he lives. Jason was entitled to continue schooling until he turned twenty-one when he would graduate.

I was on my way to Hershey Medical Center to meet Jason and Kim for an appointment with Dr. Segal. Earlier, I indicated Jason had a spinal curvature and at that time it was at thirty degree curvature. He told me if or when it reaches sixty degrees, he will consider performing a spinal fusion. We took Jason to radiology to have his back x-rayed.

Dr. Segal entered the examination room with his usual pleasant demeanor. He shook Jason's hand and asked him how he was doing. He turned around to me to say hello and he asked me how the Philadelphia sports teams are doing. I suspected he already knew because he followed all the Philadelphia teams, but it was his way of communicating and providing a calming atmosphere in the room.

He took out Jason's X-ray and placed it on the light screen. As he is pointing out the curvature of Jason's spine, which was very apparent even to me, he began to talk. "Mrs. Quate, take a look at the X-ray. You can see the curvature." He points out with a pen. "It now measures at sixty degrees. It is considered to be a serious curvature. I strongly recommend spinal infusion at this time. He is now in the critical stage where this large curvature of his spine, can cause problems with his major organs such as lungs, heart or kidneys, because of the close proximity of these organs."

I was not responding, just letting him explain everything in detail to me.

"I am not going to sugarcoat this for you. It is major surgery with risks. However, with major surgery, there is always risks. I believe Jason is strong enough and will get through this with no problems. You will see a major difference in his posture," he continued.

He showed me pictures of other patients before and after the surgery and the difference was amazing, especially how much taller they sat in their wheelchairs.

I felt I had no choice. Allen and I had already discussed the possibility of Jason having the surgery. We both decided if the curvature increased, we would agree to the surgery. I began to talk and with tears in my eyes.

"I have been watching the deterioration of his body through the years, and I need to know what is next. How many more surgical procedures are in his future? What is his prognosis for the future?"

He took my hand and said. "I understand this is difficult. However, only God knows the answers to your questions."

I looked at him and nodded as if I understood. Did I?

"I do have a recommendation. There is a new doctor on staff who is prescribing Baclofen distributed with a pump. This pump is inserted into the patient's stomach. Baclofen has been proven to control spasticity in cerebral palsy victims."

He left the room and returned with a brochure and handed it to me. "This explains the procedure in more detail. If you decide this is something you would like for Jason, call my secretary and she will schedule an appointment for an evaluation with this doctor. If you decide to go ahead with the Baclofen pump, it should be inserted before the spinal fusion is performed.

I did have a small problem with the charge nurse at the center. She was against having the pump placed. Her theory was based on the fact it was a new procedure, and she did not know anything about it and was reluctant to agree for Jason to get it. I understood her concerns since she was responsible for his daily care. However, I was clearly a risk taker and she was not. I did not see how this could hurt him. If Jason develops negative symptoms, of course it would be removed. I believed it was worth a try. I would never back away from a new procedure available that potentially would help Jason, and I certainly had no intentions of doing it now. I downloaded material from the internet and mailed it to her. I also set up an appointment with the center's doctor with the intent to show him the same material.

We met with him in his office, and before we began to defend our case, he stopped us and said, "I agree with you and I give my approval for Jason to go through the trial. After my own research on the internet, I read a medical journal article and the possibilities are amazing. The research studies prove Baclofen helps decrease spasticity but the oral form comes with side-effects. This study using a pump to directly insert the Baclofen to the spine is a fascinating theory. I believe in it and I am looking forward to seeing how it changes Jason's muscle spasticity."

I walked out of his office feeling very blessed. Jason not only had great professional support, but I was very aware of the respect I received as Jason's mother.

Allen and I decided to schedule the appointment. We saw the neurosurgeon a few weeks later, and he agreed to accept Jason in his trial. The plan was for Jason to be admitted to the hospital for a twenty-four-hour observation. He would be observed while the medicine was adjusted and checked for his response throughout the period of time.

The trial was performed. He immediately reacted positively to the medicine. The dose was adjusted several times to observe Jason's reaction. It was successful, and Jason was cleared to have the Baclofen pump inserted.

The following month, Jason again was on his way to the Hershey Medical Center, and I was with him. The pump was surgically implanted, and he returned to his room to be monitored for the next twenty-four hours. Everything appeared to work properly.

I was watching him being placed in his chair, and immediately, I could see a difference. He appeared to be much more relaxed. A computer was used to adjust the drips per minute. They were carefully monitoring the dose with the computer to help him achieve a normal range of muscle tone. When they were satisfied with Jason's muscle tone, he was cleared to be discharged. He will need to return to return every six weeks to fill the pump with more Baclofen. The pump will beep if the medicine was below a desirable amount. I was thinking to myself how funny it would be if someone was changing Jason, and they heard a beeping sound coming from his body. I knew Jason would use it to his advantage.

At first, the people who worked closely with Jason appeared to be very aware of something protruding from his stomach, and they were very cautious dressing him or moving him in positioning. They appeared to be very conscious of the pump and no longer wanted to put him on his stomach. However, after a while they began to adjust, especially with the change in Jason's muscle tone. It was much easier to dress and undress him. The physical therapist was able to perform range of motion without too much difficulty and the occupational therapist developed new goals based on his looser tone. It appeared the pump placement created a positive effect for Jason and his caregivers.

Two months later, Jason was readmitted to Hershey Medical Center for the spinal fusion surgery. All three of us drove up from Philadelphia to be with Jason to provide support and comfort.

Michael and Allen were pacing back and forth while Jason was in surgery. I was sitting quietly working on a needlepoint project to calm my nerves. Jason was taken down to the operating room at 9:00 a.m. We waited throughout the day getting updates by phone from the operating room nurse.

Normally, this procedure would not take this long. They needed to wait in the OR for the neurosurgeon to remove the pump, and then they waited again for the neurosurgeon to return to replace the pump.

We finally saw Dr. Segal walking down the hallway nine hours later. He appeared to be very wearily approaching us still in his operating room scrubs, but with a smile on his face, he announced, "Jason tolerated the procedure very well, and he is now in the recovery room. Judy, why don't you go down to see him to make sure he is okay?"

I arrived in the recovery room, and Jason was lying very still with his eyes closed. I quietly approached him and called his name. He opened his eyes and gave me his "Mommy, I am scared" pout. I picked up his hand to comfort him and asked him, "Are you feeling pain, sweetie?" With tears filling his eyes as his response, I knew he was telling me he was in pain. I asked the nurse to administer some more pain medication. She did and he peacefully fell asleep. I stayed with him holding his hand until the orderlies transferred him to his hospital room.

The next day, we are all sitting by Jason's bedside, and he appeared to be comfortable. I knew he must be in pain, but he did not tell me. After I was taught how to really communicate with Jason directly, I started to believe pain was part of his life. He did not know what life was like without pain. He believed pain was part of living. He accepted pain up to a certain level, and when he reached this level, he would let you know. He will only tell me when he has severe pain. We can all learn a lesson from this very special person!

A few minutes later, Dr. Segal entered the room. He approached Jason's bed and appeared to suddenly be agitated and started mumbling obviously to himself. He removed his jacket as he started climbing on his bed to reach under Jason. He picked him up, carried him over to his wheelchair, and placed him in it! As he was doing this, he was mumbling asking, "Why is he still in bed? I do not want him lying here. He needs to be sitting in his chair." After we recovered from his startling actions, Allen and I quickly ran over to help him get Jason settled into his chair.

He certainly startled us. We were thinking no way should he be out of bed so soon after having major surgery. Dr. Segal looked at Jason and then at us and commented, "Now look at him in his chair. What do you see different?"

We looked and I think all three of our mouths hung open in surprise. He looked like he grew at least three inches overnight. Yesterday, he was sitting in his chair looking like a child, and now he looked like a grown man. "Wow!" is all I can say! "What a difference a day makes. He is no longer my baby. He is a grown man with spastic quadriplegic cerebral palsy sitting tall in his chair with his arms loosely spread on his table, and he is smiling."

I turned around to Dr. Segal and gave him a big hug and said, "Thank you! I will forever be in your debt. You just showed all three of us how much you care."

High School Graduation

Upon discharge from the hospital, Jason's family at the center anxiously and lovingly took care of him well and he recovered without any setbacks. It was so obvious Jason has another family who loved him very much.

After his return, Jason's caregivers at the center were amazed how good he looked and how tall and distinguished he was. "He is sitting so straight in his chair and his muscle tone is so much better now that he has the pump in place." I heard this statement over and over again during my next visit.

In May of 2001, Jason graduated from high school. Jason was now twenty-one, and he was going to be a high school graduate

On May 25, 2001, the entire family from the Philadelphia area attended Jason's high school graduation. They used the Lincoln Intermediate Unit building #12 as their venue. It was a very warm. There was no air conditioning in the building, and therefore, it was very warm in the building.

The graduation program lasted about an hour. Dignitaries from the school district were there to present awards and diplomas. When Jason's name was called to approach the podium to accept his diploma, the entire room erupted with cheer because all of his family and center family were present to help celebrate Jason's accomplishment. He was wheeled over to the podium, and he very happily received his diploma and kisses from the staff, and of course, he showed his pleasure as always with a big smile.

After the graduation ceremony, the school provided a very nice reception. There was a piano player and a spread of food was laid out on a nearby table. I was standing by Jason and he appeared to be very warm and sweat was dripping down from his forehead down to his neck. He had a suit jacket on earlier, but it was quickly taken off after the ceremony. He was now in his shirt sleeves.

He was starting to get pale and shaky, and I began looking around the room for the nurse. Jason started trembling all over, and he then started having a seizure. His whole body was jerking with his eyes rolling back in his sockets. I was terrified. Jason's teachers, who were standing nearby, saw what was happening and ran over to take care of him. They moved him out of the room into the hallway and the nurse joined them soon after. He came out of the seizure after a minute. Someone placed cold towels on his forehead while one of the staff members retrieved the van and immediately placed him in the van and took him back home.

I was told this was the first time he had this type of seizure, and they contributed it to the heat and excitement of the evening.

We followed him home. We find found Jason lying in his bed resting, and he appeared to be back to normal. He was smiling and laughing with Uncle Lou's singing. He looked at me as if he was saying, "I am so sorry to ruin my party, but it was so warm and I didn't feel well." I reassured him everything was fine.

We were in our car the next day returning home. Again, my mind was wandering with unpleasant thoughts. *I watched my son have a grand mal seizure. It was a very traumatic scene, watching him shaking all over with his eyes rolling back in his sockets. There is so much to think about. Jason is now twenty-one years old, and last night's seizure proves he is deteriorating. I have to start preparing myself for the future. I feel in my heart my son knows he is getting weaker, and he is preparing himself for the inevitable. I truly believe he is accepting the changes knowing there is a better place he could go to for peace of mind where there will be no more surgeries and no more pain.*

Community Living Home

Sometime prior to 2004, we received a letter from the Director of the Skills of Central, Pennsylvania. (Several years prior, this company purchased the Children's Developmental Center). The letter was somewhat alarming. The letter informed us all clients who resided in the facility where Jason lived were going to be moved to individually handicapped accessible homes that were being built or renovated. The governor of Pennsylvania, Edward Rendell, made a proclamation and mandated all "institutions" housing the mentally retarded individuals in Pennsylvania will be closed and clients will be mainstreamed into community living.

We were invited to attend a meeting to further discuss the proposal and how they were going to implement the changes. I was fully aware Jason was labeled as a severely physically challenged client in the center. With this being noted, I was wondering how this could be implemented for Jason. However, I was willing to hear what they had to say. I needed to be reassured Jason would still have the 24/7 nursing care available to him. Allen and I definitely planned on attending the meeting with an open mind. We wanted to give them the opportunity to explain how they were going to implement this directive for Jason.

The meeting was well attended with all staff available to answer questions. I was surprised to see a large attendance of client families, some of whom I never met through all the years Jason lived there.

We were told Jason's group, the most physically severe individuals, would be the last group to move out because they were the most difficult group to manage and work through the challenges. We were reassured Jason will continue to receive 24/7 nursing care and the excellent quality care would continue. They had unofficial plans for several houses spread out through the different counties of Pennsylvania. We were given an opportunity to request what county we wanted Jason to live. We only requested he not be moved further than he was now. Since we already lived two and a half hours away, we did not want him any further than this. We also suggested, if possible, a house closer to Philadelphia.

I received a phone call from Jason's social worker a few months after the meeting. She informed me they had a house in mind for Jason and another client whose family also resides in Philadelphia. She had similar severe physical challenges as Jason and would need the same level of care as Jason. The house they had in mind was only two hours from Philadelphia. She asked me for my approval, and I granted it.

There plans were set up for four clients per house with four bedrooms. Each client would have their own bedroom. There would be two bathrooms shared between the four clients. They would have 24/7 nursing care and also 24/7 caregivers assigned to the house. This house had a large backyard with a patio, and there would be room to place an in-ground pool sometime in the future, if they desired.

I realized for the first time in sixteen years Jason, would have his own room with a window. He was a young man, and he needed his privacy. He would have his own television set and radio to listen to. After thinking through all of the arrangements securing Jason's safety, I was beginning to love the idea.

A few weeks before Jason's move, we were invited to tour the house. The renovations were completed along with the permits needed for the house to be part of a residential neighborhood as a Community Living Facility.

They had a town meeting to inform and help all the town residents to understand who would be living in the house. I was told many neighbors attended the meeting. They needed and wanted to be reassured.

This was a big concern for me because I heard horror stories about Community Living Homes in Philadelphia where neighborhood committee members absolutely refused any type of community living facility near them.. However, this was not Philadelphia, and the people seemed to be more compassionate and understanding. The few neighbors who had issues were given further details, and they finally walked away with a better understanding and were reassurred.

Michael, Allen, and I drove up that day to see Jason's new home. As we walked in and toured each room, we were feeling extremely excited for Jason. His room was fully furnished with beautiful light color furniture and bright walls. The bed was placed where he could see out the window overlooking the back yard and the trees. He would hear and see the birds chirping. He had his own television set and radio. The bathroom was handicapped accessible with a motorized lift to secure the clients in and out of the tub. The whole house was full of light and bright color walls. I knew Jason would love this house, and we were very excited for him. The staff members assigned to care for Jason were all new hired staff. They had an opportunity to work with Jason for a few weeks so they could get to know him and Jason could do the same.

Moving day finally arrived, and Jason settled into his new home and new room. I was told he had the biggest grin on his face when he entered his room and saw all his pictures and his small Hess truck collection all displayed on wall shelves. He had everything around him that was familiar, and it certainly helped him adjust quickly. Note: Poppy Quate bought Jason a new Hess truck yearly for the past fifteen years. Needless to say, he had a big collection.

My mind was burning again with building rage. "What prompted the Pennsylvania Office of Mental Health/Mental Retardation to finally realize our Jason was capable of living in a neighborhood, in a community, and in a home receiving the same quality of care he received all these year in his "institution" they paid for. I prayed to God many years ago for help so we could keep Jason at home. Why couldn't they provide funding for nursing to care for his needs to allow him to remain in his home with his family? Instead, they offered funding for him to leave our home, leave his family and only then, he was eligible for Medicaid and SSI and full-time care in an "institution." The money appropriated all these years for his care in his "institution" would have been better served for him to live in his own home. All we needed was a home with handicapped accessibility and a full-time nurse!"

Luckily, Jason's sweet personality never changed when he moved away from his family home because this was how special he was. However, we were denied the opportunity to have our child and brother at home with us. We were denied the chance to watch Jason grow up, and we missed the special times when he goofed around, played tricks with his friends, attended boy scouts, went to amusement parks, and attended special picnics and school activities. It did occur to me how inadequate it was back then. It was the state of culture in 1987, and there was no one in politics advocating the rights for the special needs child.

Michael and Amanda's Wedding

The day was July 17, 2004. A very special day indeed; Michael was getting married to Amanda. Jason was going to be "honorary best man." He will be placed in front of the pews in order for him to have a good view of the ceremony. My nephew Barry was the official best man.

Michael met Amanda at a local franchise restaurant. Michael worked at this restaurant since he was sixteen years old. Amanda had been working at the same restaurant as a server while she was attending college.

My motherly instincts led me to believe Michael was looking for a woman who would be his best friend, a loving wife, and a good mother. He most definitely found these qualities in Amanda.

Amanda is driven both professionally and personally. I believe she was looking for the same qualities in a man, and she found the right man. She is a goal-oriented young woman who knows what she wants in life. She wants a good man as a partner, best friend, and a good father for her future children. In addition, she is driven to build a career of her dreams. They are suited for each other. She drives Michael to succeed, and Michael's quiet but strong personality keeps her focused and composed.

Amanda asked to meet Jason before the wedding. We all drove up to visit him. We introduced Amanda to Jason, and he just looked at her. While we were sitting in the living room chatting, I was watching Jason. He would occasionally look over at Amanda. I was wondering what he was thinking about. Does he understand a man and a woman meeting, falling in love, and getting married?

Through the years, I would occasionally allow myself to imagine Jason as a "normal" child and young man. I imagined him taller than Michael. I would allow my mind to imagine Jason being a flirt and having many girlfriends. I allowed myself the privilege of dreaming that Jason and Michael would be the best of friends. They most likely would have normal sibling rivalries such as competing with each other with sports, girls, and education. If Michael had the opportunity to develop a brotherly relationship with Jason, I believe Michael would not have been as passive and shy as a child. However, it was just my imagination. One has the right to dream to pacify their inner soul.

We were at the church with the priest and rabbi waiting for the couple to walk down the aisle. Amanda was a beautiful bride, and Michael was so handsome in his tuxedo. I saw Michael looking so tenderly at Amanda as she was walking toward him with her father down the aisle. Jason was sitting in front of the pews in his wheelchair beaming. The service began with both the priest and rabbi sharing their individual prayers as tradition calls. The rabbi placed the glass by Michael's feet, and he aggressively stamped his foot down on the glass, and it shatters in pieces; immediately, the guests yelled out, "Mazel Tov." My family began to sing "Mazel Tov" repeatedly as they stood up clapping along with their singing. This is a traditional verse sung after the glass is broken. The entire room joined in to sing and clap as well. I looked at Jason, and he was screeching with joy. Oh yes; he knew and felt the excitement in the room and was very aware of what was happening.

We reserved a room for Jason at a nearby hotel so he could rest in order to attend the evening festivities. Jason had the opportunity to be with the close family as the photographer took the portraits.

Jason returned to attend the cocktail hour. No, he did not have a drink, but I bet he would have loved one! Several of my cousins drove/flew in from around the country, and this was their first opportunity meeting Jason. I was so thrilled for them to have this chance to meet him.

Just before it was announced dinner was ready, Kim approached us with Jason to say good-bye. They had a long drive home and wanted to stop by the hotel first to change Jason and feed him before they get him settled into the van. I was thankful someone was willing to use their personal time on a weekend to drive Jason to his brother's wedding.

Moving

Michael and Amanda found an apartment in Bucks County, Pennsylvania, which was forty-five minutes north of Philadelphia. We were still living in Philadelphia.

The city and neighborhood we both grew up in and raised our children was changing. It was sad. Both Allen and I lived here our entire life and loved the closeness of people and enjoyed the safety we felt for many years. However, time changed with our beloved neighborhood changing as well.

Our friends/neighbors were very close. They decided to place their house up for sale, and they all moved eventually. We began to feel left behind. We missed Michael. Michael urged us to move near him. He missed us also.

I was still working and was planning to continue working until 2010 when I would retire. Allen was also working. We found a beautiful home in Bucks County about ten minutes from Michael and Amanda.

In August of 2005, we moved out of the home where we raised Michael and Jason. We had so many memories. I realized I wasn't leaving the memories behind. The memories will always be with me. However, because we both grew up in this neighborhood, it was very emotional. This was the only place we knew, for both of us, since childhood.

I had five more years until I retired. I was commuting to downtown Philadelphia, and I rode the train to and from work every day. Each way was forty-five minutes, but I used the time wisely. I either listened to audio books or music from my iPod or talked to my fellow passengers who took the same train with me every day. The difficulty with this daily journey on the train was getting up at the crack of dawn at 4:00 so I could catch the early 5:35 train to be at work by 7:15. My work day ended at 3:30, and I arrived home at 5:00. It was a very long day, and I was starting to feel the effects both mentally and physically.

Double Pneumonia

Jason was twenty-eight, and it was November, 2006. The one question I had on my mind now that he was getting older was, what was Jason's life expectancy? I would often ask professionals and their should be answer would always be, "God only knows." Of course I knew this, but I needed to prepare myself for the inevitable. I knew God gave Jason to me for a reason. God knew I was a bud, and I needed something in my life to help me blossom. He knew me to be a strong woman who was spiritual, and he gave me Jason to help me reach my full potential. I now know I accepted what God gave me and Jason helped me become a better person both spiritually and intellectually.

When I was a young woman and newly married, I had a very low self-esteem with no self-confidence. Since then, I've grown to be a self-confident, strong-minded, spiritual woman and capable of believing I could do anything I wanted to if I really believed I could. (This book is a perfect example).

God knew what he was doing when he picked me to be Jason's mother and advocate. I received praises many times throughout the years from Jason's doctors, nurses, therapists, and the staff at Skills of Central PA. I always found them difficult to accept because I saw myself as his mother with a job to do. My response after being praised always was, "I am just a mother who is taking care of her disabled son. What makes me different?" Their responses to me were, "You are more than just a mother, you are his advocate and you are doing a great job."

After many years, I now understand why they complimented me. I now believe I did the best job I could do for Jason, and I am proud of myself. I jumped through hoops to be the person I am today. Life taught me a valuable lesson. It is my dream that after reading Jason's story and you are struggling with a special needs child, you will walk away with a better education and understanding of what it takes to be a good advocate and caregiver for your child. You just have to believe in yourself.

I am at work on a chilly November day working quietly in my office. The end of the fiscal year was now over. Traditionally, the end of September was very pressure-driven and trying time to clear out last year's finances and begin the New Year. The New Year budget began October 1.

My phone rings. "Bureau of Prisons, this is Judy, can I help you?"

"Mrs. Quate this is Jason's nurse. Jason is on his way to York General Hospital. We found him in his bed this morning with vomit on his sheets. His nail beds were blue along with his skin color. The paramedics arrived and immediately gave him oxygen and quickly rushed him to the hospital."

I am listening to her, but I knew he aspirated and probably developed aspirating pneumonia based on what she just told me.

"Mrs. Quate, it looks pretty serious, and we are all very upset," she continued.

"I will wait until the doctors have a chance to evaluate him before I call the hospital," I responded.

I no longer panic. If I did, I would lose control and it would keep me from being focused. In the past, I would wait until I could talk to the doctor evaluating him before I made any decisions.

I waited for an hour and then called and spoke to the nurse in the emergency ward at York General Hospital. She told me he was immediately intubated because his oxygen level was very low, and he was now in the radiology department getting a chest X-ray. I didn't need or want to hear anything more. He was intubated and that meant he was in serious condition.

I entered George's office. He saw the expression on my face and immediately wanted to know what was wrong. I told him what happened, and he responded, "Leave now and don't worry about the work on your desk; just leave!"

I called Michael and Allen, and we arranged to meet at our house. I took the next train home, and on the train, I sat staring in space, trying to keep myself calm.

As soon as the three of us gathered at our house, we immediately left for York General Hospital. We arrived and found Jason was transferred to the intensive care unit. We headed to his room. Because of Jason's disabilities, the head nurse allowed the three of us to sit around Jason's bed. She felt it would comfort him to know his family was with him, and I agreed.

The attending doctor arrived who was a pulmonary specialist. After introductions, he began to explain Jason's condition.

"Jason has developed double aspirating pneumonia. His lungs are very weak, and his blood oxygen level is extremely low that prompted us to immediately intubate him. We transferred him here because he is in severe distress and needs to be watched carefully."

It was late in the afternoon, and we were not going anywhere. We were sitting through the night to be with Jason. I sat by his side and held his hand, and he just looked at me with very sad eyes. He knew he was very sick. The nurses provided two additional chairs that transformed into beds. Michael found a sofa to spread out on in the ICU waiting room. We didn't sleep much, and Michael wandered in and out of his room occasionally throughout the night to check on his brother. It was a very difficult night for all of us. Jason was sleeping on and off during the night but was holding his own.

In the morning, we decided I would return home with Michael and Allen. We all had the feeling this would be a long hospital stay. I went home with them only to pack a suitcase and then left in my car to return to Jason.

I slept by Jason's side in his room for the remainder of the week. I wanted to be available in order to communicate with the doctors and nurses and other specialists to keep myself informed of his condition.

I called George to ask for a leave of absence. I didn't know how long I was going to be out of work, but we both knew I would not leave Jason. He supported me 100 percent and told me not to worry about anything. If I were to run out of sick or personal time, he would request the personnel department to seek donations from the staff. He told me my coworkers were all very concerned, and they send their love and support. I spoke to Pamela a few times. She always helped me through any problems with her supportive personality and by being a good friend.

The week alone with Jason consisted of daily visits from doctors, nurses, and clergy who were assigned to Jason's care. Jason was assigned a social worker who stopped by occasionally to check on me and sit and talk, just to keep me company. I mostly stayed by his side; occasionally holding his hand so he knew I was with him. When I left the room to get meals or take care of personal needs, I would tell Jason I was returning very shortly and his eyes expressed a smile like he was saying, "Okay, Mom." There were no changes that week. Jason's lungs were very weak and only time would tell if they would survive the trauma.

Allen returned the following Sunday, and we sat together with Jason all day. He convinced me to return home with him that night and come back the next day. At first, I was reluctant to leave Jason, but eventually, I realized I needed some time away from Jason. The long hours in the car provided the down time to listen to soft music or an audio book to keep my mind occupied. Spending time at home, eating dinner with Allen, and sleeping in my own bed at night was giving me the break I needed so I could find the strength to stay with Jason all day.

Three weeks passed with no changes in Jason's condition. He was still on the respirator. I received a phone call from Pennie. She wanted to schedule a meeting for the next day and coordinated it with Jason's nurse, house supervisor, the clergy representative from the hospital, and the hospital social worker.

I anxiously waited for all of them to arrive because it scared me not knowing the purpose of the meeting. We all gathered in Jason's room. Pennie started the discussion.

"Due to the severe condition Jason is in, it is prudent at this time to discuss DNR [Do Not Resuscitate] action. We will respect your decision in this matter. However, by law, because Jason is considered to be a ward of this state, there are laws we need to abide by."

I responded immediately and spoke very clearly, "I do not want Jason to suffer. If or when he stops breathing after the respirator is removed, I want DNR to be respected." I further said, "I feel he suffered enough his entire life, and if he stops breathing, it is in God's hands."

Note: I cannot recall the exact law stated during this meeting related to 2006 DNR law for wards of the State of Pennsylvania. However, I do know everyone in attendance at the meeting were respectful of my opinion, and it never became an issue.

When the meeting ended and everyone left, the clergy representative stayed behind to talk with me. He began by praising me for the way I conducted myself at the meeting, and he was amazed by my strength and endurance. I reminded him I was Jason's advocate for many years and my son, and I have a special relationship without verbal communication. I also told him I know what Jason wants by looking into his eyes. He believed me and responded, "Only a mom who had the responsibility you had through the years would truly understand this, and I believe God is supporting you and Jason." He further said, "Only God knows when it is time to take Jason." I concurred.

The following week, Jason continued to remain stable but in critical condition. The pulmonary doctor stopped by to see Jason. He checked his vital signs along with his blood work and then sat down to talk with me.

"It is my recommendation to cut into Jason's trachea to perform a tracheostomy. This is an artificial opening for Jason to breath. By doing this, we can attempt to remove the respirator to see if he can breathe room air. If we need to replace the respirator, we will no longer have to risk placing the tube through his esophagus. He is in a fragile condition, and his esophagus and lungs are weak with disease. We can attach the respirator directly to the opening in his trachea. I sat there and listened, but my thoughts were again going in so many different places. I prayed to God for guidance and asked him to take my son. I was beginning to believe Jason had reached his life expectancy, and it is now his time to leave this earth. He has been a brave boy for twenty-eight years, but if he has to live with a tube attached to his neck to help him breathe, he no longer has a quality of life. However, these are my personal prayers and my responsibility as his mother was to continue to help him. After relaying this conversation from the doctor on the phone with both Michael and Allen, we unanimously came to the conclusion to allow the doctor to perform the procedure.

He tolerated the procedure and returned to his room with the tracheotomy in place along with the respirator. A few days later, the doctor removed the respirator, and Jason successfully was breathing on his own with the support of oxygen. It was apparent this last bout of pneumonia had taken its toll on Jason's lungs and left them in a weakened condition.

Pennie visited one day while Jason and I were sitting quietly watching television. We were happy to see her, and Jason smiled when she walked in the door. Unfortunately, she brought bad news. The home Jason was living in was unable to support Jason with a tracheotomy. It required him to receive specialized nursing care not available at this time. She wanted me to know she tried everything she could to find the bed for Jason in another home, but she was unsuccessful. She was visibly upset and told me everyone at Jason's home was devastated. I told her I understood.

We now have another hurdle to jump. We needed to find a new home for Jason. It occurred to me we could look for a home in Bucks County where we live. A nursing facility would be a suitable place for Jason to live and there was a wonderful facility just ten minutes from us. I spoke to the social worker who was assigned to Jason to help find a placement. She was familiar with the nursing home I told her about and would contact them to start the initial paperwork to get him a bed there. Jason was transferred to a medical floor awaiting discharge.

I decided to return to work. Jason was now in stable condition, and I had been out of work for over a month and needed to return. I used up all of my accrued leave and my fellow staff members so kindly donated the additional leave I needed in order to continue to receive my salary. I would always be in debt to those who graciously donated their hard working time to me.

I returned to work and my life returned to a somewhat normal state. I was working closely with the social worker at the hospital to help quicken the move to the nursing home.

I had to leave Jason alone in the hospital. I was not comfortable, but there are times when you need to make a decision you do not like. I learned something sitting with Jason during the past month. I no longer can control what happens. I know God had taken over his care and whatever happens, it was in his hands and Jason's.

God Calls for Jason

On a cold wintry day, December 22, 2006, I was sitting at my desk, in my office, working. Many of my coworkers were away for the holidays. It was quiet in the office, and I enjoyed the peace. George was in his office and was planning on leaving for his vacation the next day and would be out for two weeks spending time with his family during the holidays.

I was listening to one of my favorite music tracks on my iPod and keying and processing bills. I was suddenly startled when the phone rang. I did not expect interruptions because everyone was away for the holidays. I was surprised. I picked up the receiver, "Bureau of Prisons, this is Judy; may I help you?"

An unfamiliar voice responded, and I was forced to listen carefully because he had a heavy accent. I managed to hear him say, "Is this Mrs. Quate?"

"Yes, it is," I responded.

"I am the doctor on call caring for your son at York General Hospital. I am very sorry to inform you your son Jason passed away at 11:05 this morning."

I think I just heard him tell me Jason passed away, but I needed to be sure and asked him again, "What did you just say?"

"Mrs. Quate, your son passed away. I am so sorry," he repeated.

He continued to say some jargon regarding pre-planned questions one would ask when they are telling a family member someone died.

"Will you give permission for an autopsy? If not, you need to make arrangements to pick up his body."

I heard him say, "Your son Jason died," and everything after that was muffled. I was processing his words; the words I knew I would hear one day.

After twenty-eight years loving, caring, and laughing with my dear son, he was now gone. In my heart, I knew this day was coming, but I was not allowing myself to believe it. He was my life, and now, he had been taken by God to a better place.

"Mrs. Quate, are you still there? Mrs. Quate?"

"Yes, I am still on the phone, and I am sorry but your words are difficult for me to process."

"I understand, and again, I am very sorry for your loss."

I suddenly processed what he said and responded to him, "No, I do not authorize an autopsy because of religious beliefs. Yes, I will be in touch with our funeral director, and he will call you."

I ended the call and sat for a while trying to process what he told me. "I was not able to cry. There were no tears. I had no feelings. Maybe I am in shock? What does one do when they are in shock?"

I finally got up from my chair and started walking toward George's office. I am thinking, *I suppose I need to tell him I have to go home.*

I entered his office, and he was on the phone. Apparently, I must have looked very pale and had an expression on my face that told him he needed to end his call quickly. He hung up the phone and walked over to me.

I had my hands on my face and told him, "I just received a phone call and the doctor told me Jason died."

He guided me toward the chair in his office and squatted down and asked me what happened. I told him, still without tears. He didn't know what to do for me. He asked me if I called Allen yet, and he offered to call him for me.

"I did not call anyone," I answered. "Yes, I think I need to make some phone calls."

He walked me back to my office and allowed me some privacy so I could call my family. I reached Allen, and he was as shocked as I was. He told me he was leaving the office now and would meet me at home. I called Michael, but he did not answer his phone. I knew Amanda was teaching her classroom, and I didn't want to disturb her with this news now.

George wanted to drive me home, but I insisted I could take the train. He did insist on driving me to the train station. I started cleaning my desk and gathered my coat and purse. Several of my coworkers heard the news from George and they stopped by to console me.

I met George outside our building, and he drove me to the train station. As he pulled the car up to the curb, he asked me to call him with details of the funeral, and I promised I would. While I was waiting for my train, an announcement over the public speaker informed me the train I was waiting for will be delayed and at this time should be they do not know how long. This was not an unusual occurrence with these trains. However, this was not want I needed to hear that day..

I was sitting on the bench trying to decide what I could do. I could take another train, but I would need someone to pick me up and take me to the station where my car was parked. I didn't want to ask Allen. I was already concerned about him driving the long distance from work after hearing our tragic news. Suddenly, I heard my name and looked up and standing in front of me was a coworker from another department. He was waiting for another train that was not delayed and he offered for me to take his train, and he would drive me to my station to pick up my car. He did not know about Jason. I told him, and he was very upset. He told me not to worry, and offered to drive me directly home. He didn't want me to drive my car in the state I was in.

The train arrived, and we sat together on the train toward the train station. We didn't talk. I insisted he drop me off at my train station. I was only fifteen minutes away from the train station, and I wanted to pick up my car.

I arrived home and Allen was already home. We sat and held each other for a long time without talking, just consoling each other.

I attempted to call Michael and still did not get an answer. I called Amanda, and she was in her car on her way home. I asked her to pull over, and I told her what happened.

"Oh my god! I thought he was getting better! What happened?" she cried out.

I asked her to find Michael because I could not get him on the phone. She promised she would.

Michael and Amanda arrived an hour later, and we started making the necessary arrangements. Allen contacted a friend who ran a family owned funeral pallor. We previously arranged Jason's funeral a few years ago with him. He told Allen he will make all the arrangements and will call us back with details. About an hour later, he called to say a few of his staff members were now on their way to York General Hospital to pick up Jason's body.

Allen and I spent most of the night remembering the beautiful child we had and how amazing he was. We laughed at the funny stories and mourned the life he endured, but we both agreed that finally Jason was in peace. We believed he was met at heaven's door "walking" through the gates talking up a storm. He was now walking and talking and most importantly, no longer in pain.

I believed this was what he wanted all along. He waited for me to leave his side so I would not watch him die. He didn't want to say good-bye to me. It would hurt too much for both of us. This was our special child, and he left this world in his terms.

The funeral was planned for December 26, 2006. Many of our family and friends were there to support us. All of Jason's friends and family from the center drove down from York County to say good-bye to their friend. The room was fully packed, and we were so proud and thankful for all the support we received.

The immediate family were invited to see Jason before the casket was closed. Amanda took one look at him and quickly left the room crying. She told me later it was too difficult to see him lying in the casket because he looked like Michael lying there, and she couldn't bear it.

He did look like Michael lying in the casket, and it was unbearable to me as well. I was upset because he didn't look like himself. Our friend, the undertaker, came over to Allen and me as we were holding each other and reminded me why I did not recognize Jason.

"It is because he isn't smiling."

"Yes, you are right; Jason always has a smile on his face."

After looking at Jason lying peacefully, it also occurred to me he looked different because I never saw Jason without his familiar spastic muscles with the rigid neck and head stiffness. Yes, the Baclofen did help loosen him somewhat, but he still had some stiffness. It was so typical to see him with his tight muscles contouring his body for so many years.

We were listening to the rabbi speak so kindly about our child. He reminded everyone that Jason was very special and that we should not cry because he was now in peace with God.

I felt the obligation to talk to our friends and family. I wanted them to know what kind of person Jason was and how he changed so many lives by being so special. I needed to tell them he had a purpose to be a great son, brother, and friend and that he loved his life and did not know or understand he was different.

Life goes on. The funeral and the Shiva observances are over, and we needed to continue our life without our dear son. Returning to work was difficult. My life now had changed. I no longer received the phone calls about routine procedures such as meetings and doctor appointments.

The Skills of Central PA was planning a memorial to honor Jason's life. It was going to be on January 15, 2007, at their main headquarters in Hanover, Pennsylvania.

Memorial

The Skills of Central PA held a memorial for Jason on January 15, 2007. It was held in their main office building in Hanover, Pennsylvania. The room was packed with all of Jason's friends, staff and family, including Allen, Michael, Amanda, and I.

Opening remarks were made by Pennie Spalding. If you recall, Pennie was the first person we met when we arrived at the Children's Developmental Center many years ago. She knew Jason for twenty years. Her words in her opening remarks were so beautiful and touching, especially because she knew Jason so well. I attached below what she read to the attendees.

> We have come together here today for three reasons, to mourn the loss of a friend, to celebrate his life and to talk about what knowing him has meant to us. I want to thank all of you for coming, because you are here, means that Jason has touched you all. Not only has he touched those of you in this room, but those who could not come; because it is too painful, they chose to honor him in a different way, or because they are sad, nonetheless, these are more lives he has touched. There are many more people who got to know him in the years he has been with us. There are the physicians, the staff, the teachers, the visitors, consumers, the consumers' family, and the staff families. We would

need a room ten times bigger to accommodate them all. He was connected to us and us to him, and not only him, but his family, his family's family, his family's friends, his friends at home and the list goes on.

In 1979, two baby boys were born at Albert Einstein Center in Philadelphia, one of whom weighed a little over three pounds and was fifteen inches long. He was whisked away to the Intensive Care Unit from the delivery room, and so from that point, marked the story of Jason's life and not in negative terms. What I mean is he was on the go. While in the hospital he was transferred several times and finally came home several months later at a whopping seven pounds in weight and twenty inches in length. Listening to his mother talk to a whole room full of doctors at the York Hospital in recent months, commanding in a gentle way their attention, I was impressed how she held them in the palm of her hand, speaking very eloquently about what she wanted for her son. She learned this kind of negotiating early and she learned it well.

When Jason went into the hospital we spent Thanksgiving worrying about him and making sure he received the care he needed. We needed to make some difficult decisions, the whole team, and when I mean team, I mean mom, dad, and everyone. It turned out Jason had other plans and slipped away on December 22, 2006. His death left us all in a little bit of a shock, considering how the last time I saw him he was laughing at Evelyn and I because we had been hurrying to get to his room to meet with the doctors and hospital staff and had to run down a big hill in heels. Jason, who I thought was snoozing, started to laugh at that. That is how I will remember him, that adorable smile, that wonderful personality.

Not only did we get to have Jason as one of our own for almost 20 years, but we had his family. Never did I speak with his mother without her reminding me they only wanted the best for Jason, or without telling me she trusted us with him. She felt we were his extended family, what an honor.

If you read any official paperwork on Jason you would know that he had a diagnosis with about fifteen things on it, a list of surgeries, appointments and procedures several pages long, and a file this high, but he was not a label, he was not a condition, he was a little boy who grew up into a sweet natured teenager, and into a lovely young adult.

So ladies and gentlemen, if you are worrying that you can't find the right word today, don't. It's not the content of the eulogy, or the length, or the perfect recall of biographical details that matters; it's the heart and soul that is important. I know Jason will always be in our hearts and souls forever.

Another speaker was introduced, Sue Trimmer. She read a letter that is meant to be from Jason to all of us in attendance at his memorial. It was so beautifully written and so touching I wanted to share it with you here.

As my caregivers and friends, I think too often you underestimated the power of touch, a smile, a kind word, a listening ear, an honest compliment, or the smallest act of caring; all of which have the potential to turn a life around. In today's workforce it's easy to make a buck. It's a lot tougher to make a difference. But each and every one of you who unselfishly gave of yourselves during my 20 years of residence at the Abbottstown Service Center, Skills of Central Pa, and my "very own" new home, was an important part of the quality of life that I was so very blessed to experience.

With all certainly, please know that my spirit is alive and with you in this room today. And if you just close your eyes, you will surely see the beautiful smile that was always on my face, a smile that was so uniquely mine because you cared. In the next few weeks ahead find strength in each other as you continue to bring that same experience to the other thirty-nine members of my extended family. Till we meet again, thanks so much, and take care.

We were all touched with the warmth and love we felt in the room with Jason's memorial. It will be something I certainly will never forget.

Letter from a Special Friend

I have one more letter that was written and read at Jason's memorial. It was a letter written by "Jerry." He knew Jason for many years as he describes in his letter. I knew he had a special relationship with Jason, and this letter spells their relationship out very clearly. He was unable to attend the memorial because it hurt too much to face his death; therefore, another member of the staff read it. We were all so touched by his words and how he so innocently expressed his love for our son, it deserved a special place in Jason's book, and of course, its own chapter.

> Hey Jason, it's me, Jerry. I've been thinking about you a lot lately. I really miss you!! I remember when I first met you. It was quite a few years ago. I had just started at the center. It was my first week "on the floor" and I was being oriented by a young woman named Terri. We were in Room #8 and she was explaining a goal one of the residents in this room was working on. His name was Jason also. He had blond hair and was very outgoing. He had a goal where he was to help another resident to maneuver themselves while on a scooter board. Terri placed "Jason L" on his scooter board and he knew exactly what to do. He scooted down the hall to Room #5 and knocked on the door. Terri and I followed, of course. When I entered the room I saw a

very young boy with dark hair about eight years old on his belly on a scooter board. That was you, Jason and that was the first time I met you. Jason L scooted over to you and placed his hand on yours and gently moved it. He started laughing and was a little vocal…you in turn smiled and laughed also. I thought that this goal was cool especially since it involved interaction between both of you guys and you both seemed to enjoy hanging out together.

Eventually I became regular staff in Room #8. I remember the daily routine of taking Jason L up the hall to visit you to work on his goal to help you maneuver your scooter board. Remember I use to tell ya, "Jason L and I will see ya tomorrow—same time, same place!"

A few years past and I remember eventually I became your regular staff Jason. I remember putting you on your wedge and the nurse would come in and do percussion on your back. Usually it was your friend Cindy S that would do this. I know this would always make you feel better because once Cindy was done you didn't cough as much. I really think though that what you really enjoyed was spending time with Cindy. I enjoyed watching the interaction between you and Cindy. I learned a lot too! She'd carry on with you and you'd smile and laugh. I also remember Cindy had a secret stash of your favorite candy. Of course, you were still eating at this time and we were given the okay to offer you this snack every night at snack time. I use to melt them in the microwave and as soon as I told you "here's your peanut butter cup" you'd open up your mouth. I never saw you eat so fast!

Along with your upper respiratory problems you had more medical problems to deal with Jas. I remember seeing you in discomfort with your hips and legs. I guess that's why you had your cool bed that would help the pressure. Plus you had operations to help with this and of course, your pump. I remember telling new staff that if out of the blue you start making "beeping" sounds, not to worry! That just means your pump is getting low on medication.

Of course this never happened. You had your visits to the hospital to make sure everything was working okay with your pump. Anyway, Jason, God gave you a lot to endure with all your medical problems but you were strong and carried these "crosses" well.

One thing that was always important to me Jason, besides the daily chores, working on goals, doing personal hygiene, etc., was making sure you were comfortable. Remember me every two hours, repositioning you in your bed. I use to place you on your wedge or scooter board (before you got the pump). I'm sure you will never forget your leg splints. I use to put that on your leg every night at 9:00 PM, and then we had your least favorite—hand splints. I remember at first how you would clench your fingers together telling me you didn't want them on. I would wait a little while, you relaxed, and then I would try again. After doing this every night, you eventually just let me put them on your hands with no problems. Some nights it was easier, especially if you were sleeping!! A few times I could tell you were not feeling well because you really resisted when I tried putting them on. I believe a couple of times you even resisted so much that a few of the straps broke off!! Eventually, lucky for you, I believe the splints were discontinued after they kept making marks on your hands and arms.

I believe what I will always think of and remember about you, Jason, is your smile and laugh. You had such a great sense of humor. One of your favorite types of movies on TV was the horror ones. You would always laugh hysterically when you heard a girl scream at the top of her lungs during one of these movies. You would also laugh like this when you heard me sing to "Roy" and "Jarrod" in Room #6 while they were listening to the "Sound of Music" soundtrack. Of course when I sing in your room, "In the Jungle the Lion Sleeps Tonight" you'd laugh hysterically. Maybe that was because I was singing the real high pitched part of the song!! You always enjoyed your music! I remember one staff, and friend of yours, Bill C, he used to come in and play "MMMBop" by Hansen or just your favorite 50s or 60s music and you'd laugh and smile. One specific time when you laughed hysterically, some staff won't let me forget about this one, was when I was working a first shift. Most staff is usually tired in the morning. Well, I had two cups of coffee and I didn't want you to be late for breakfast. So after I put you in your wheelchair, I raced you up the hall and into the dining room while I made screeching noises. The staff just stared and you were smiling and laughing. You enjoyed it. That's all that counted to me! We did have a lot of good times, didn't we Jason?

On the more serious level though, I'll never forget when after working with you as your regular staff for a few years, I had a hard decision to make and once I made this decision it was so hard to tell you about it. I knew we would all be eventually going into community homes and I had to decide where/which home to go to. I eventually chose the community home closest to where I live. I also had the opportunity to switch my regular room which was your room to going to the rooms with the residents in which I would be going with in the new community home. Anyways, I'll never forget you and your roommates: Roy, Brian and Matt. I put all four of you in a semi-circle to tell each of you my future plans. This was the hardest thing I ever had to do and I was nervous. After I explained this I remember Jason, you just sat still and stared. I came up to you and asked you what you thought and you smiled. I knew everything was okay. Now in the future they eventually moved you into one of the other rooms with Matt and finally the day came for you to move to your community house. I was happy to finally see you and your housemates (three ladies—lucky you Jason!) last spring-summer. I hope you enjoyed your community home Jason. It's been a goal of so many staff to finally see you and your friends being in these houses. You all deserved it. Anyway,

Jason I remember saying "Hi" to you (after not seeing you for a good few months). I started walking in front of your new wheelchair, as I was saying "Hi" to you. It was great, because once you saw me; you gave me a great big smile!! *That meant* a lot to me Jason. I remember saying to you that you were looking good and that you definitely were getting some good feedings. I believe this was the last time I saw you Jason but I'll never forget that smile you gave me!

Finally Jason. You definitely touched my heart buddy. Another time I had a difficult time telling you something was when I told you Brian had died. You sat still in your wheelchair and stared. Then I saw your lower lip quiver and I saw tears coming out of your eyes and running down your cheek. I just gave you a hug and told you everything was okay and that Brian is in Heaven with God. Then you smiled and seemed okay. You definitely were a smart young man, Jason. Of course, Jason, now you are with Brian and Roy. I'm sure they were both there to meet you like I said. Jason I am going to miss you but I'll always remember your smile and laugh. I enjoyed so much working with you and I learned so much from you. Enjoy your "new life" with God in Heaven. Tell Roy and Brian I said "Hi" and that I miss them. Save a place for me up there. I love ya… your friend Jerry."

I am speechless. There is nothing more to say. Jerry said it all with his honesty and with so much love for my son. Wherever you are, Jerry, may God bless you for being you.

Remarks from Facebook Support Group Members

Below you will find remarks from members of my Facebook Support Groups, who wanted to add a few words of their own.

Denise Ruiz's story:

> I am frustrated because the funds available in my state for programs and activities for my son are not available where he receives his treatments. This is because they are not under the state contract. I am not free to choose where my son is to be treated based on my needs for location and the quality of care I choose for my son. I do receive respite care but the hours allocated to my son per year are not rolled over, if I don't use them up in the current year. This is just an example of the red tape I deal with in order to receive help.

Raelene Boudreau's story:

> My daughter was six weeks old and was in the Regional Intensive Care Neonatal Unit at the Children's Hospital in Cincinnati, Ohio. I was celebrating my daughter's six week of surviving and she was doing very well! Two days later Hannah took a bad turn. They ran tests but still

had no clue as to what was wrong with her. It appeared Hannah was giving up the fight. I was by myself with no support and trying to cope with the unknown at this time. I worked in the mornings so I would have gas money to get back and forth to the hospital to spend my afternoons and a good deal of the night holding onto my fragile, weak daughter. Somehow I held it together. On Friday of that week, my daughter was barely alive. She couldn't open her eyes, cry, or even squeeze my thumb. I prayed out loud hoping that God would hear me. At that very moment her heart monitor started beeping loudly as her heart raced! She cried out with a loud squealing cry and the tears flowed down her cheeks! It was a miracle. I truly believed that God was testing my faith. It was God's faith in Hannah and me that kept me going.

Hannah is now a special needs child and I need the support for her care for which I am not getting from my state of Indiana where I live now. Unfortunately our state is far behind the times in funding the special needs child. They do not share information regarding available funding for homecare, equipment or availability of Medicaid. When Hannah was an infant I applied for Medicaid and never heard a response until a few years ago when I found out they didn't have the application. It appears to me my state doesn't want families to know about available funding. Many families are lost until someone put us in the path that has the information. I was told last year that Hannah doesn't qualify for a home health aide because there is no respite care funding available. I asked who do I call to request this assistance and I didn't receive a reply.

Luckily a few years ago a pediatric unit for special needs opened in our area. It is in a building set up for geriatric care, but they have one floor devoted to pediatric care. This has been a God-send for our family and other needed families. There was nothing in our area set up for respite or permanent care before this unit opened. I feel our state does not respect the families with special needs children. It is a shame because it appears they do not believe our kids are worth investing in. However, they are our beautiful angels, a gift from God who entrusted them to us. Hannah's big smile is contagious along with her laughter and she touches our lives and so many others who care for her.

Garth Wheeler's story:

I wrote this poem five years after Timothy was born. We were told Timothy would not live past one year but he lived much longer. He could not talk or walk but could see. When he passed I donated his eyes to two other people that were born blind which gave them site for them to see the world they live in. I always wondered what Timothy was thinking. This is what inspired me to write this poem.

I Am the Child

I am the child who cannot talk.
You often pity me; I see it in your eyes.
You wonder how much I am aware of — I see
that as well.
I am aware of much, whether you
are happy or sad or fearful,
Patient or impatient, full of love and desire
Or, if you are just doing your duty by me.
I marvel at your frustration, knowing
mine to be far greater,
For I cannot express myself or my needs as you do.

You cannot conceive my isolation,
so complete it is at times.
I do not gift you with clever conversation, cute remarks
to be laughed over and repeated.
I do not give you answers to your everyday questions,

Responses over my well-being, sharing my needs,
Or, comments about the world about me.

I do not give you rewards as defined by the world's
standards—great strides in
Development, that you can credit yourself;
I do not give you understanding as you know it.
What I give you is so much more valuable — I give you
instead opportunities.
Opportunities to discover the depth
of your character, not mine.
The depth of your love, your commitment,
your patience, your abilities;
The opportunity to explore your spirit more deeply than
you imagined possible.
I drive you further than you would ever go on your own,
working harder,
Seeking answers to your many questions with no answers.
I am the child who cannot talk.

I am the child who cannot walk.
The world seems to pass me by.
You see the longing in my eyes to get out of this chair, to
run and play like other children.
There is much you take for granted.
I want the toys on the shelf, I need to go to the
bathroom, and oh I've dropped my fork again.
I am dependent on you in these ways.
My gift to you is to make you more
aware of your great fortune,
Your healthy back and legs, your ability to do for yourself.
Sometimes people appear not to notice me;
I always notice them.
I feel not so much envy as desire, desire to stand upright,
To put one foot in front of the other, to be independent.
I give you awareness.
I am the child who cannot walk.

I am the child who is mentally impaired.
I don't learn easily, if you judge me by the world's
measuring stick,
What I do know is infinite joy in simple things.
I am not burdened as you are with the strife's and
conflicts of a more complicated life.
My gift to you is to grant you the freedom
to enjoy things as a child,
To teach you how much your arms around me mean, to
give you love.
I give you the gift of simplicity.
I am the child who is mentally impaired.

I am the disabled child.
I am your teacher. If you allow me,
I will teach you what is really important in life.
I will give you and teach you unconditional love.
I gift you with my innocent trust, my
dependency upon you.
I teach you about how precious this life is and about not
taking things for granted.
I teach you about forgetting your own needs and desires
and dreams.
I teach you giving.
Most of all I teach you hope and faith.
I was the disabled child...
I was the disabled child who could not see, I was the
disabled child who could not talk, and I was the disabled
child that could not walk.

Epilogue

I continued throughout this book to say periodically I felt Jason was not mentally retarded. It now occurs to me I need to say something that may have been misunderstood. Please understand I would never love Jason less if he was mentally retarded. Jason had so many complex issues, the fact that he expressed some intelligence without verbal skills was something I was able to cling to, and it gave me hope.

I love all special needs children. Through the years I met many mentally retarded children who were full of compassion and love. I have an older cousin who is mentally retarded but he has been living alone for years, and I am so proud of him. Each child with special needs is unique in their own way, and this is how I saw my son—a unique individual with special needs.

I would like to tell you a story about a dream I recently had that really touched me greatly. In this dream, I was visiting Jason, and he was having fun with his friends, laughing, and just hanging out. I approached him to say good-bye, and he lifted his arms to hug me that caused me to cry.

I was startled suddenly, awakened from my dream, by my iPod alarm playing "The Circle of Life," from the Lion King, written by Sir Elton John. This was Jason's favorite song as I was told, and it was played at his memorial service.

I have several points to emphasize. To begin with, I did not cry at Jason's funeral. The defense mechanism I created for years kept me from showing emotion, even at his funeral. Another point to mention, Jason was never physically able to lift his arms to hug me. I was never hugged by me son. The last point is clearly mind blowing, how ironic, of all the songs I have on my iPod, which are over a thousand songs, I was awakened with Jason's favorite.

I interpret this dream to believe Jason was reaching out to me from heaven and thanking me for telling his story, and he believes his story will make the difference we both want.

Recently my grandson and I had a conversation about death. He is only five years old but he has the wisdom far beyond his age. His GG Pop passed away so death was on his mind. I told him his Uncle Jason died. His middle name is Jason in honor of his uncle. He told me Uncle Jason is now in heaven with his GG Pop and they are not sleeping up there. They are living in heaven now. How sweet and wise my grandson is and I hugged him and thanked him for his loving thoughts.

I love the time I spend with both of my grandchildren and will always cherish the memories. As I watch them play I think about how I now have the privilege to just sit and watch children play. I missed this opportunity with my boys many years earlier.

Afterword

It is now time to get on my soapbox and give a "yell out" to the powers that be who I hope are reading this book.

Our special needs children today are crying out for your support. Their parents need guidance and more programs that are not full of red tape bureaucracy. I understand our needs may be lost due to other important issues of today. However, if someone would just think about these beautiful children who are in need of help, open up your heart and help them please.

The people who run our country do not know our plight unless we tell them. This book is a source to spread the word. Please help Jason and I make it happen. Thank you!

Editor's Review

Judith,

First of all, I commend your courage and brave heart to bring back all those memories, especially the painful and difficult ones. As I was reading your book, I can feel your overwhelming love for your family and especially for Jason. He is blessed to have a mother as superb as you. The people who praise you for your efforts are right. You didn't just function as Jason's mother. You were an advocate, a best friend, a nurse—more than a mother can offer.

You made the right decision in putting Jason's story into writing. A lot of people would be able to relate to this, especially families who have a physically or mentally challenged member. Your book will help them realize how important it is to be able to communicate with a person like Jason; that communication is very important, even if there are no words said.

You have written your book in a very simple way, but it never failed to give out tons of emotions. Every chapter has a beautiful story, and it gives important lessons to be learned.

I would love to meet Jason should he have been alive. He really was someone special despite being unable to communicate verbally. Nonetheless, I know he had lived a good and happy life. And despite all what happened, you remained strong and loving.

I hope to have that courage, strong will, and confidence that you have when God will give me more and much difficult trials.

It is always up to you if you would want to follow these suggestions as you are the author of this book. More specific notes are found within the story, and I hope they will make sense. I have done some direct changes, but there are some points that you need to decide on.

Thank you for allowing us to work with you and your lovely story. We are truly honored, and I personally enjoyed your book. I wish and pray for the success of this book and your future endeavors.

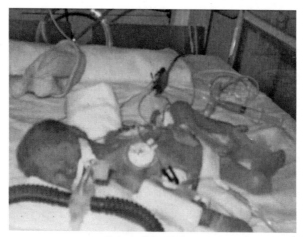

Jason in NICU

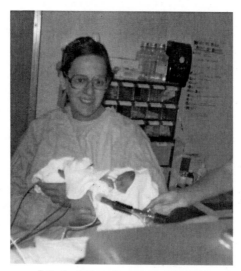

Me holding Jason in NICU

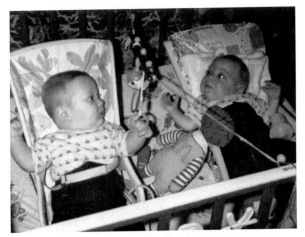

Michael and Jason

First Birthday Party

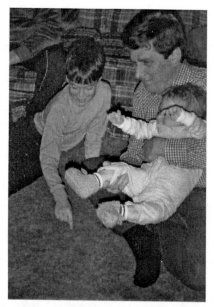

Dad, Jason and Barry playing footbal

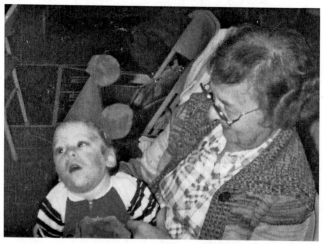

My Mom holding Jason

Jasons portrait at 8 months old

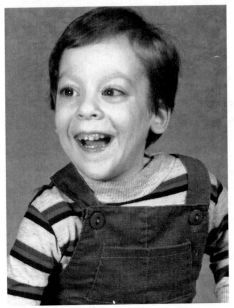

Jasons portrait at 18 months old

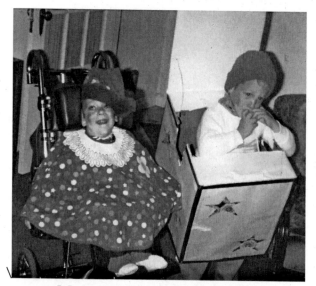

Michael and Jason at Halloween

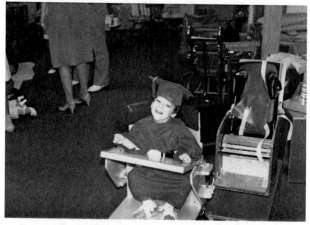

Jason Graduates Early Intervention Program

Michael, Jason, Dad, Rena and Barry

My Dad with Jason

Jason's new home

Jason's new room

Our family visiting Jason

Michael holding Jason

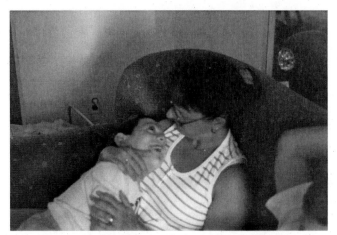

Me and Jason

Me and Michael

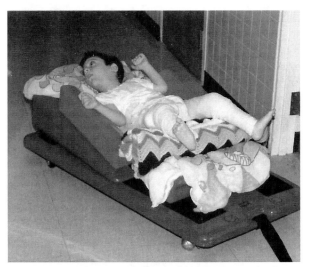

Jason after hip surgery

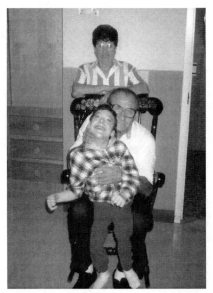

Bubby and Poppy Quate with Jason

Meladye holding Jason

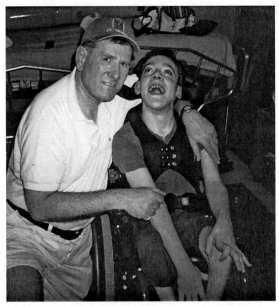

Dad with Jason

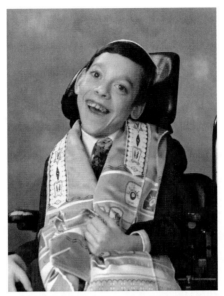

Jason's Bar Mitzvah Portrait

Jason's High School Graduation Portrait

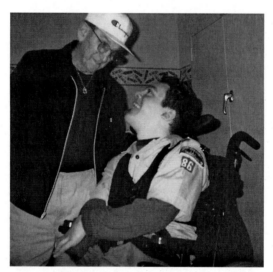

Uncle Lou singing to Jason